BUS SYSTEMS FOR THE FUTURE
Achieving Sustainable Transport Worldwide

INTERNATIONAL ENERGY AGENCY

INTERNATIONAL ENERGY AGENCY
9, rue de la Fédération,
75739 Paris, cedex 15, France

ORGANISATION FOR
ECONOMIC CO-OPERATION
AND DEVELOPMENT

The International Energy Agency (IEA) is an autonomous body which was established in November 1974 within the framework of the Organisation for Economic Co-operation and Development (OECD) to implement an international energy programme.

It carries out a comprehensive programme of energy co-operation among twenty-six* of the OECD's thirty Member countries. The basic aims of the IEA are:

- to maintain and improve systems for coping with oil supply disruptions;

- to promote rational energy policies in a global context through co-operative relations with non-member countries, industry and international organisations;

- to operate a permanent information system on the international oil market;

- to improve the world's energy supply and demand structure by developing alternative energy sources and increasing the efficiency of energy use;

- to assist in the integration of environmental and energy policies.

IEA Member countries: Australia, Austria, Belgium, Canada, the Czech Republic, Denmark, Finland, France, Germany, Greece, Hungary, Ireland, Italy, Japan, the Republic of Korea, Luxembourg, the Netherlands, New Zealand, Norway, Portugal, Spain, Sweden, Switzerland, Turkey, the United Kingdom, the United States. The European Commission also takes part in the work of the IEA.

Pursuant to Article 1 of the Convention signed in Paris on 14th December 1960, and which came into force on 30th September 1961, the Organisation for Economic Co-operation and Development (OECD) shall promote policies designed:

- to achieve the highest sustainable economic growth and employment and a rising standard of living in Member countries, while maintaining financial stability, and thus to contribute to the development of the world economy;

- to contribute to sound economic expansion in Member as well as non-member countries in the process of economic development; and

- to contribute to the expansion of world trade on a multilateral, non-discriminatory basis in accordance with international obligations.

The original Member countries of the OECD are Austria, Belgium, Canada, Denmark, France, Germany, Greece, Iceland, Ireland, Italy, Luxembourg, the Netherlands, Norway, Portugal, Spain, Sweden, Switzerland, Turkey, the United Kingdom and the United States. The following countries became Members subsequently through accession at the dates indicated hereafter: Japan (28th April 1964), Finland (28th January 1969), Australia (7th June 1971), New Zealand (29th May 1973), Mexico (18th May 1994), the Czech Republic (21st December 1995), Hungary (7th May 1996), Poland (22nd November 1996), the Republic of Korea (12th December 1996) and Slovakia (28th September 2000). The Commission of the European Communities takes part in the work of the OECD (Article 13 of the OECD Convention).

FOREWORD

Rapidly increasing traffic congestion, air pollution, and sprawl are jeopardising the ability of the developing world's premier cities to achieve sustainability. These problems, present in most large urban areas of developing countries, also account for a substantial share of the expected increase in world oil use and CO_2 emissions over the next twenty years.

Near-term bus system improvements in these cities – before cars become dominant – could be among the most important and most cost-effective approaches for achieving transport sustainability. Compared to urban transport systems dominated by private vehicles, bus-dominated systems result in much less traffic congestion, lower energy use and emissions, and improved mobility for all social and economic classes.

New bus technologies are also emerging that can dramatically reduce emissions and oil use from buses themselves.

This book shows how better bus systems and bus technologies can put urban transportation on a more sustainable path around the world.

Robert Priddle,
IEA Executive Director

ACKNOWLEDGEMENTS

This publication is the product of an IEA study undertaken by the Office of Energy Efficiency, Technology and R&D under the direction of Marianne Haug, and supervised by Carmen Difiglio, Head of the Energy Technology Policy Division. The study was coordinated by Lew Fulton and Lee Schipper. The book was co-authored by Lew Fulton, Jeffrey Hardy, Lee Schipper, and Aaron Golub. Other individuals who provided important contributions include Lloyd Wright, ITDP (New York), Dana Lowell, NYCT (New York), Peter Danielsson, Volvo Bus (Sweden), Jean Cadu, Shell (UK), Karl Fjellstrom, GTZ (Surabaya), Roland Wong, BEMP (Dhaka), Dinesh Mohan, IIT (Delhi), Bambang Susantano, Pelangi (Jakarta), Florencia Serrannia, STE (Mexico), Claudio de Senna Frederico, Secretaria de Estado dos Transportes Metropolitanos (CPG, Sao Paulo), and Oscar Diaz, formerly of the Mayor's Office of the City of Bogota.

The IEA would also like to express its appreciation to the following individuals for their advice and support to develop the programme of analysis that led to this publication: Karen Peabody O'Brien and J. Q. Zhang, both formerly of W. Alton Jones Foundation, David Rodgers, US Department of Energy, and Glenda Menges, Homeland Foundation.

Assistance with editing and preparation of the manuscript was provided by Chris Henze, Scott Sullivan, and Sally Wilkinson. Production assistance was provided by Loretta Ravera, Muriel Custodio and Fiona Davies.

The cover photo of Bogota's TransMilenio bus system courtesy of Peter Danielsson, Volvo Bus Corp.

TABLE OF CONTENTS

LIST OF TABLES

LIST OF FIGURES

EXECUTIVE SUMMARY

Around the world, cities face enormous problems of transport sustainability. Rapidly increasing populations and vehicle use have created gridlock and sprawl, even in very poor cities, as well as rapid growth in oil use and unacceptably high levels of air pollution. This book shows how better bus systems, incorporating new approaches to system design and new technologies, can put urban transportation on a more sustainable path. It covers three areas: new bus systems, new bus technologies, and profiles of a number of cities around the world that are tackling very difficult traffic-related problems.

Compared to cities dominated by small private vehicles, those with well-designed bus systems have much less traffic congestion, lower pollutant and CO_2 emissions, and offer better mobility for all social and economic classes. Bus systems in the developing world carry a large share of urban travellers but are responsible for only a small part of traffic congestion, energy use and pollution. This is because reasonably full buses are inherently efficient – in terms of both road space and fuel use per passenger kilometre. Even "dirty" buses emit far less pollution and CO_2 emissions per passenger-kilometre than most other types of vehicles. But transit shares of travel are declining in many cities and conditions are worsening. Changing these trends and moving toward more sustainable transport is imperative. Our analysis indicates that for a city like Delhi, there is a 100% difference in oil use and CO_2 emissions between a future transport system dominated by travel in high-quality bus systems and one that is dominated by private vehicles.

While many new technologies are emerging to improve buses, perhaps the most important story to be told is that the systems in which buses operate can be dramatically improved. Bus transit can be a premier form of urban travel. A new paradigm in delivering bus services, becoming known as *bus rapid transit,* is being developed in a number of cities, particularly in Latin America, and shows promise for revolutionizing bus systems around the world. Getting buses out of traffic, increasing their average speeds, improving their reliability and convenience, and increasing system capacities can ensure high ridership levels and increase the profitability of systems.

Once buses are moving and providing a service that attracts riders, then the question of bus technology does indeed become important. A dizzying array of new bus propulsion systems and fuels has emerged in recent years, but Chapter 3 lays out the key facts for several of the most important options. Policy makers and bus operators in both the developing and developed world may find this discussion useful, with sections on "clean diesel", biodiesel, gaseous fuels, hybrid-electric engines, and fuel cells. The concluding section illustrates the wide range of costs of different options and provides a technology "ladder" – a pathway toward cleaner buses that starts with inexpensive, relatively straight-forward measures and reaches much more expensive and complex measures, such as fuel cells, that may eventually become cost-effective.

All in all, the package of improvements described in this book, and being tested and implemented in various cities around the world, holds the potential to make all cities more efficient, cleaner, less gridlocked and more sustainable. But it will not be easy. It will require technical assistance and the transfer of experience and learning from successful cities to those just starting out. Perhaps most of all it will require political will.

KEY MESSAGES

Each additional bus, if reasonably full, provides large social benefits through mode-switching and a reduction in traffic. Regardless of whether a bus is "clean" or "dirty", if it is reasonably full it can displace anywhere from 5 to 50 other motorised vehicles, including often very dirty two-wheelers as well as cars. In some developing cities the primary displacement is of high-emission motorcycles and scooters. The fuel savings, CO_2 reductions and air pollutant reductions from switching to bus travel can be large – possibly much larger than those from making a fuel change or technology upgrade to the bus itself.

The collective impact of bus system reform on world oil use can be large. Transport drives oil demand and transport is growing three times faster in developing countries than in developed countries. Since bus system reform will substantially cut oil use in the large urban centres of developing countries, where transport demand is growing quickly, the collective impact of sustainable bus transport can be as important as any other strategy to reduce world oil demand.

Development of "Bus Rapid Transit" (BRT) systems in Latin America opens a new era in low-cost, high-quality transit. Bus systems in cities like Curitiba (Brazil) and Bogota (Colombia), with dedicated lanes, large-capacity buses, and specialised bus stations that allow pre-board ticketing and fast boarding, are a quantum improvement over standard bus systems. Average travel times have been reduced substantially and the overall travel experience for most riders greatly improved. The system in Bogota, though only three years old and still under development, already has one of the highest ridership rates in the world. Most large cities would benefit greatly from bus rapid transit systems.

The institutional, financial and operational aspects of bus systems must be strengthened. In many poor cities, most buses are run by small independent companies, some of which survive from day to day. These companies are rarely able to make major investments. Systems must be reformed to improve service and profitability, by moving from "bus versus bus" competition on the same route to competition for a licence to serve entire routes. The level of service required for the entire route should be specified in the contract, and provision of this service should be assisted by supporting policies, such as adequate fares.

Testing of new bus systems in "demonstration corridors" is an important step. Pilot or demonstration projects can create the "seed" that later grows into a fully established system of bus rapid transit routes. Demonstration projects can include dedicated bus lanes, improved bus stops and terminals and new ways of licensing and regulating bus services on the route. They can also offer a showcase for advanced technologies, or simply modern buses.

New, low-cost bus-system technologies can help. When lanes and entire corridors are given over to buses, bus travel becomes increasingly attractive. With such additional features as bus priority treatment at intersections and traffic signals, buses can become a premium form of urban travel, rather than a last resort. Global positioning systems (GPS) to track bus position and relay this information to travellers in real time, so they know when buses will arrive, are also becoming cost-effective. "Smart card" ticketing systems can allow easy transfers and multiple trips with one electronic fare card. In such cases, technology "leap-frogging" makes good sense for many cities in the developing world.

Transit-system improvements pave the way for bus-technology improvements. If bus companies are to justify the expense of investing in new-technology buses, those buses must earn higher revenues than current buses. Revenues can be increased through fuller buses (carrying more passengers per kilometre), faster buses (more kilometres covered per day, and more passenger boardings) and higher fares. Increasing bus ridership requires system improvements and policies that encourage public transit. Similarly, speeds can be increased by system improvements, such as dedicated bus lanes. Higher fares may be justified once the quality of bus travel improves. All of these steps may help increase the revenues generated by each bus. This is critical to enable transit agencies and bus companies to afford better buses with better emissions-control systems, and in some cases to pay for alternative-fuel infrastructure.

Bus operators should gradually "move up the ladder" to advanced bus technologies. Fuel-cell buses and hybrids are too expensive today for most developing countries. But there are many lower-cost steps that can be taken to obtain cleaner, more efficient buses. Strategies to clean up existing buses quickly include better bus maintenance and improvements in fuel quality. Incremental improvements to the design of diesel engines, control systems and after-treatment systems (in conjunction with a shift to low-sulphur diesel fuel) can reduce diesel emissions dramatically. In some cities, it may make sense to concentrate on moving to alternative fuels such as compressed natural gas or liquid petroleum gas. This depends on the availability and cost of these fuels and fuel-delivery infrastructure. It also depends on the availability of affordable alternative-fuel buses. In other cities, it may be better to focus on cleaning up diesel fuels and buses, and eventually move to advanced diesel hybrid-electric buses. Some day, most buses may run on hydrogen, but it is still too early for most cities to worry about developing hydrogen refuelling infrastructure. Bus operators need to gain experience by taking incremental steps up the "technology ladder".

Field tests of different options and in-situ data-gathering are essential. Using emissions factors and models from one city to simulate emissions in another is unsatisfactory. Each city needs to understand it's own emissions patterns, how different vehicles affect air quality, and what changes are most important. Part of this process includes testing various vehicles and technologies under local conditions. A well- designed plan to establish baseline conditions and estimate the impacts of alternative measures is an important part of any process to develop better bus systems and introduce new bus technologies.

Improved buses and bus systems should be part of a comprehensive strategy. Improving buses and bus systems will help increase the bus share of passenger travel in cities around the world. But unless strong policies to dampen the growth in car travel and, in many places, motorcycle travel are *also* applied, the fight for sustainable transport will be a losing battle. Increasing vehicle and fuel taxes, strict land-use controls and limits and higher fees on parking are important to ensure a sustainable urban transport future. Equally important is integrating transit systems into a broader package of mobility for all types of travellers, for example non-motorised vehicle lanes. Pedestrians and bicyclists are important users of transit, if they can get to it. Finally, all travel is rooted in the electric-drive structure of a city. Electric-drive development should be geared toward avoiding car-dependence and putting important destinations close to public transit stations (and vice versa).

The IEA's six case studies show that improving bus transit systems is possible, but not simple. It is complicated by the many stakeholders in each city, each with different points of view and degrees of influence; and it is complicated by the often confusing array of government agencies with some say in what initiatives occur and how they occur. Still, in all six of the cities reviewed some progress is being made to improve bus transit systems. But it will be difficult for cities to "go-it-alone". International support and technical assistance, especially from those cities that have been the most successful, will be needed to speed progress.

INTRODUCTION

The IEA projects that over the next 20 years energy demand growth in transport will be greater than in all other end-use sectors. Transport's share of total energy use will increase from 28% in 1997 to 31% in 2020[1]. Despite efforts to use alternative fuels, oil will continue to dominate the sector. Transport will account for more than half the world's oil demand in 2020 (Figure 1.1). Besides the energy security and sustainability implications of this dependence on oil, transport will also generate roughly one-fourth of the world's energy-related CO_2 emissions. These trends extend beyond the OECD. The IEA projects that growth in oil use and greenhouse gas (GHG) emissions from developing countries will far outstrip that from the developed world over the next 20 years. Oil use in transport is expected to grow three times faster in developing countries than in OECD countries (Figure 1.2).

Figure 1.1 World Oil Consumption: Transport and Total

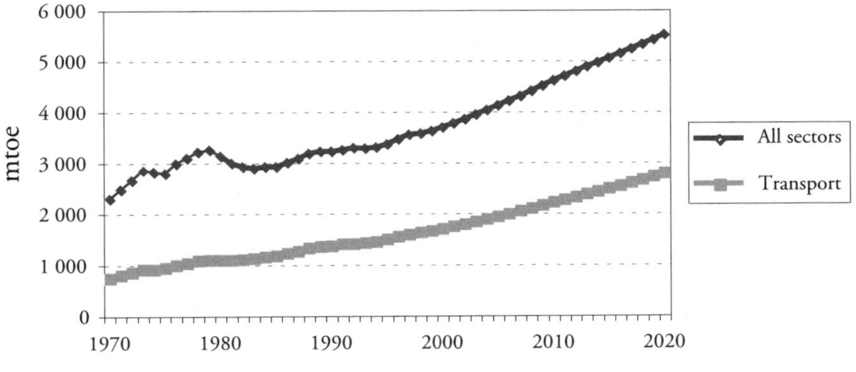

Source: IEA, 2000

---

1   The IEA *World Energy Outlook 2000* forecasts 2.4% annual growth over this period.

Figure 1.2 Forecast Growth in Oil Use in Transport, Developing and OECD Countries

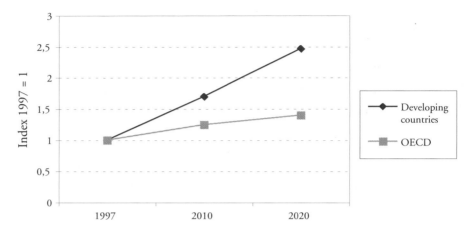

Source: IEA, 2000

The next decades will also witness staggering population growth. Within five years, half the world's population will live in cities. By 2030, the urban population will reach 4.9 billion – 60% of the world's population (Figure 1.3). Moreover, nearly all population growth will be in the cities of developing countries, whose population will double to nearly 4 billion by 2030 – about the size of the developing world's total population in 1990.

Figure 1.3 Estimated and Projected World Population, 1950-2030

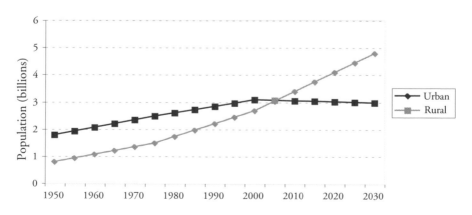

Source: UN Population Division, 2000.

These trends raise troubling questions. Can urban centres continue to endure increasing emissions from vehicle tailpipes? Can the atmosphere safely absorb massive releases of greenhouse gases? How can living conditions improve for the millions of people in urban centres? Will declining mobility strangle commerce and grind cities to a halt?

Industrialised countries generally have well-developed transport systems and have made progress toward solving pollution problems. In developing countries, increases in per capita income and escalating population growth have contributed to rapidly rising demand for transportation and energy without commensurate investment in transport infrastructure or emissions control.

IEA countries must continue to curb GHG and other polluting emissions and also expand their efforts to close the widening gap between demand for mobility and what transport systems are able to provide. By moving people and goods more efficiently and improving vehicle technologies and fuels, transport can become more sustainable.

Developing countries need access to environmentally sound technologies. Technology co-operation can only succeed through joint efforts by enterprises and governments, by suppliers of technology and by its recipients. Governments, the private sector, and research and development facilities must take steps now to ensure sustainable transport.

Collaboration and transfer of technologies – as well as ideas – must also take place between developing countries. Radically new approaches to developing and operating bus transit systems are emerging, but currently exist mainly in Latin America. These successes must now be transferred to Africa, South Asia and South-east Asia. The developed world can assist by providing linkages between different cities and regions and facilitating co-operation and learning.

URBAN PUBLIC TRANSPORT IN DEVELOPING COUNTRIES: POTENTIAL AND PROBLEMS

Transport systems are the life blood of cities, providing mobility and access that is critical to most activities. But many transport systems are beginning to threaten the very liveability of the cities they serve. This is occurring even in cities where car ownership is still very low, because they are ill-equipped to handle rapidly increasing private-vehicle traffic. The resulting traffic congestion has a direct effect on economic growth, not to mention safety, noise and air pollution. The problems are particularly acute in the developing world's largest cities. Swollen populations and high densities of vehicles of all types mean major congestion, slow travel, high exposure to polluted air and high mortality rates from traffic accidents (World Bank, 1996).

At the same time, growing incomes lead more and more individuals to choose forms of travel that add to these problems. Traditional non-motorised transportation, such as walking and bicycling, give way to motorised transport – first buses, then often motorcycles and finally cars. Urban transport systems are built around the automobile, requiring an extensive roadway system and large amounts of land, and stimulating high per-capita energy use. Los Angeles, perhaps a symbol of the logical conclusion of this progression, is now attempting to "retrofit" its sprawling landscape with a mass-transit system, but this is difficult to do when there are as many cars as driving-age residents. In many cities, however, it may still be possible to steer toward efficient, cost-effective transport systems – centred on high-quality bus transit – that serve all segments of society and curb the rush to private vehicles.

Urban transport in the developing world is already a major contributor to local pollution and CO_2 emissions. Motor vehicles account for more than half the emissions of carbon monoxide, hydrocarbons and nitrogen oxide in many developing cities. They typically produce a smaller, but increasing, share of particulates. As for CO_2, the IEA projects that in the next 20 years, transport in developing countries will contribute about 60% of the growth in global CO_2 emissions from transport and about 15% of the growth in global CO_2 emissions from all energy sectors (IEA, 2000).

The stakes are high. CO_2 emissions from transport in a developing city dominated by buses could be half the amount of a city dominated by private cars. Figure 1.4 shows 1990 data for New Delhi and two possible scenarios for 2020. There is a 100% difference in the city's transport energy use and CO_2 emissions depending on whether buses in that year carry 75% of motorised trips and are large and fairly full (average load of 60 passengers), or if they only carry 40% of motorised trips and are smaller and/or emptier (35 passengers).

Figure 1.4 Two Future Visions For Delhi[2]

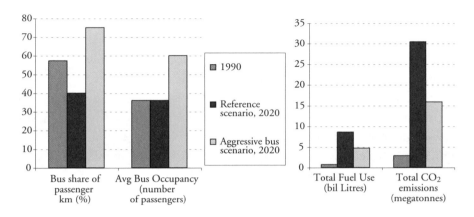

High emission growth rates have been occurring despite the fact that, in many developing cities, a large share of urban passenger transport is already borne by buses. In such cities, buses account for half or more of all motorised passenger trips, while taking up only a small fraction of road space. Forty to fifty years ago, cities in the developed world had similar shares of bus transport. In European cities, buses carried as much as half of all traffic in urban areas until the 1950s or 1960s. In most cities this was followed by a steady decline in bus travel. Buses have been displaced in part by metros, but increasingly by private cars.

In Mexico City, Bangkok and many other cities, middle-income citizens are deserting buses and other forms of collective transport in favour of individual modes of transport. The same trend is evident even in very poor cities, such as Delhi, where travel by private vehicles (including two-wheel scooters, three-wheel taxis and cars) is growing much faster than bus use. Just how fast, and how far, this new trend goes will depend on many factors, such as rates of income growth, the price of automobiles and the way cities grow. It will also depend – crucially – on the quality and financial health of mass-transit systems – especially bus systems.

2   Source: Scenarios developed by IEA based on similar scenarios from Bose and Sperling, 2001.

WHY URBAN TRANSIT BUSES?

Why is it important to preserve, improve and expand bus systems? The answer is simple: they offer the most affordable, cost-effective, space-efficient and environmentally friendly mode of motorised travel. While rail travel is also an important sustainable transport mode, rail systems have several disadvantages compared to bus systems. Rail is expensive; even light-rail systems can cost up to 10 times as much per kilometre as bus systems[3]. New rail systems often require new rights-of-way, a process that can involve engineering difficulties and political pain. Moreover, it can take many years to develop rail systems. In some respects rail offers advantages, such as greater capacity and faster speeds. But some recent advances in bus systems could close this performance gap.

Can recent trends be reversed? Can bus systems become a "growth area" in developing cities? The experience of a few cities suggests that they can, and that the benefits of doing so are substantial. In Curitiba, Brazil, an advanced-design, high-capacity bus system has grown up along with the city over the past three decades, and now carries a high share of all motorised travel. Citizens of that relatively wealthy city simply use their cars less than other Brazilians. The success of the bus system in Curitiba has spurred other South American cities, such as Porto Alegre, Bogota and Quito, to develop similar high-capacity systems.

In much of the developing world, however, buses are seen as inefficient and hazardous as well as major sources of pollution and noise. City authorities are just beginning to become aware of new types of efficient, clean and affordable buses that can improve this image and maintain or even increase their share of trips, while improving total mobility. Such a vision can become reality if bus systems are modified to offer better speed, service and convenience than personal vehicles.

Research for this book found several common, interlocking factors:

- ■ In many large cities in the developing world, traffic is gridlocked, even though car ownership is still very low – generally fewer than 100 cars

---

3   A report by the US General Accounting office (GAO, 2001) estimates that average construction costs per kilometre for bus systems range from 2% of rail transit for buses in bus lanes in urban arterial streets to about 39% of rail for dedicated busway systems.

per 1000 people and in some cities fewer than 50. Each additional bus avoids the need for many smaller vehicles, and provides mobility for dozens of people.

■ Urban air quality is often a critical environmental and health problem in developing countries. Better bus systems can dramatically reduce total vehicle pollution.

■ Virtually all of the various alternative fuels and advanced propulsion technologies under development have been tested and used in transit buses, which make an excellent platform for testing. For many alternative fuels, infrastructure is undeveloped and unfamiliar to consumers. This will be less of a problem for transit vehicles since they are centrally fuelled by staff that can be trained to maintain vehicles properly and handle fuel safely.

■ For transit agencies under pressure to lessen the environmental impact of their vehicles, advanced technologies and alternative fuels may provide attractive options for dealing with air and noise pollution.

■ International organisations like the World Bank, the United Nations Development Program and others are working to find sustainable transportation solutions for developing countries. Development agencies and the international community of transportation experts are two of the major audiences for this book.

THE IMPORTANCE OF GETTING BUSES MOVING

Perhaps the single most important factor in creating successful bus systems is getting buses out of congested traffic. Increasing bus speeds is very important for several reasons. It is critical to providing an improved service that encourages ridership, and it helps raise revenues – which in turn affects the quality and type of bus that can be employed. Slow buses travel fewer kilometres each day and therefore carry fewer (fare-paying) passengers.

Faster-moving buses, with shorter waiting times and more frequent, reliable service, can dramatically increase ridership. Cities like Curitiba have shown that even car owners will ride the bus – if the bus can match their car's speed and reliability. In cities with bad traffic congestion and low average speeds for *all* vehicle types, getting buses moving can give them a clear edge over other forms of travel. Chapter 2 elaborates how this can be achieved.

THE ROLE OF NEW BUS TECHNOLOGIES

A variety of new bus propulsion technologies and systems are being developed that could make important contributions to energy savings, improving air quality and reducing CO_2 emissions, as well as provide superior service to travellers. Chapter 3 reviews conventional and advanced propulsion systems for buses, including "clean" diesel and alternative fuels. It also compares cost and emission impacts for cities in both developed and developing countries.

A major question addressed in this chapter is how much it will cost, and how difficult it will be, for cities in developing countries to adopt complex new technologies and systems. Some bus companies do not have the resources to properly maintain even their current, relatively basic, buses. After reviewing individual technologies and fuels, Chapter 3 concludes with a discussion of these issues, and how companies might move up the "technology ladder", starting from relatively simple and low-cost improvements before adopting more complex and more expensive approaches.

All of the fuels and vehicle technologies we review have strengths and weaknesses, and different options may be better for different cities, transit agencies and bus companies. We spell out the various attributes of each choice and consider the situations in which each might be a strong option.

CITY EXPERIENCES: IEA'S CASE STUDIES

The IEA worked with various cities around the world that are attempting to develop better bus systems (note that cities *already* possessing improved systems are discussed in Chapter 2). The objectives for each city were to understand the current transportation, and in particular bus transit, situation. We review recent initiatives undertaken to seek transit-related improvements, and discuss what else could be done and what obstacles stand in the way. Chapter 4 presents case studies of six cities.

The case studies show that improving bus transit systems is certainly possible, but not simple; it is complicated by the many stakeholders in each city, each with different points of view and degrees of influence; and it is complicated by the often confusing array of government agencies with some say in what initiatives occur and how they occur. Still, in all six of the cities reviewed some progress is being made to improve bus transit systems. Perhaps more importantly, each city has begun to develop a framework and plan for moving its entire transport system toward greater sustainability. But it will be difficult for cities to "go-it-alone". International support and technical assistance, especially from those cities that have been the most successful, will be needed to speed progress.

BUS SYSTEMS

This chapter investigates a number of aspects of bus systems, focusing especially on the potential benefits of bus rapid transit (BRT) systems. The reader is referred to more comprehensive treatments of other transit system options in several of the references, such as the recent transport strategy documents published by the World Bank (World Bank, 2001).

BUS RAPID TRANSIT SYSTEMS

There are many types of bus transit systems, including road/rail systems (such as trolley systems). There are also several types of dedicated rail systems such as metros. Three basic types of roadway bus systems are:

- buses that operate in general traffic, with no priority,

- buses that receive limited priority, such as bus lanes and at traffic signals, and

- buses that operate on dedicated infrastructure such as busways, with minimal interaction with general road traffic.

Systems that emphasise priority for and rapid movement of buses have become known in recent years as "bus rapid transit" (BRT) or "busway" systems (see box). Such systems have emerged as an important alternative to rail systems for providing rapid transit, and have been implemented in a number of cities, particularly in Latin America. The extent of dedicated infrastructure and the level of sophistication of different systems vary considerably. In some cases, the priority treatment of buses is little more than a road lane with pavement markings indicating the lane is for buses only. In "true" BRT systems, entire roadways are given over to buses, in some cases including grade separation ("flyovers") at intersections.

BRT systems can compete with rail systems in terms of passenger carrying capacity (passengers moved per hour, per direction). A recent review of rapid transit options undertaken for the World Bank (Halcrow Fox, 2000) provides the basis for the following classification scheme for rail and BRT (or busway) systems (Table 2.1).

What is Bus Rapid Transit?

Bus Rapid Transit is high-quality, customer-orientated transit that delivers fast, comfortable and low-cost urban mobility. – Lloyd Wright, ITDP.

BRT systems have some or all of the following elements; many of these also can make a valuable contribution to improving regular bus service:

- Dedicated bus corridors with strong physical separation from other traffic lanes.
- Modern bus stops that are more like bus "stations", with pre-board ticketing and comfortable waiting areas.
- Multi-door buses that "dock" with bus stations to allow rapid boarding and alighting.
- Large, high capacity, comfortable buses, preferably low-emission.
- Differentiated services such as local and express buses.
- Bus prioritisation at intersections either as signal priority or physical avoidance (e.g., underpasses).
- Co-ordination with operators of smaller buses and paratransit vehicles to create new feeder services to the bus stations.
- Integrated ticketing that allows free transfers, if possible across transit companies and modes (bus, tram, metro).
- Use of GPS or other locator technologies with a central control area that manages bus location at all times and facilitates rapid reaction to problems.
- Real-time information displays on expected bus arrival times.
- Good station access for taxis, pedestrians and cyclists, and adequate storage facilities for bikes.
- New regimes for bus licensing, regulation and compensation of operators.
- Land-use reform to encourage higher densities close to BRT stations.
- Park and ride lots for stations outside the urban core.
- Well-designed handicap access, including ability for wheelchair passengers to quickly board buses.
- Excellence in customer service that includes clean, comfortable and safe facilities, good information and helpful staff.
- A sophisticated marketing strategy that encompasses branding, positioning and advertising.

TABLE 2.1 BUSWAY AND RAIL TRANSIT SYSTEM CHARACTERISTICS

Characteristic	Busway	Light-rail transit	Metro	Suburban rail
Current applications	Becoming widespread in Latin America	Widespread in Europe, few in developing countries	Widespread, especially in Europe and North America	Widespread, especially in Europe and North America
Segregation	Mostly at-grade	Mostly at-grade	Mostly elevated or underground	Mostly at-grade
Space requirement	2-4 lanes taken from existing road	2-3 lanes taken from existing road	Little impact on existing road	Usually separate from roadway corridors
Flexibility	Flexible in both implementation and operation, robust operationally	Limited flexibility, somewhat risky in financial terms	Inflexible and financially risky	Inflexible and somewhat risky
Direct impact on traffic (apart from mode-switching benefits)	Depends on design/available space in roadway corridor	Depends on design/available space in roadway corridor	Does not take space away from roadway	Depends on design/location, but usually does not take away space
Integration with existing public transit system	Usually a straightforward upgrade of bus operations; some bus and paratransit routes may need rerouting to establish feeder system	Depending on design/location, may displace some existing bus transit operations; some rerouting to establish feeder system may be needed	Depending on design/location, may displace some existing bus transit operations; some rerouting to establish feeder system may be needed	Depending on design/location, may displace some existing bus transit operations; some rerouting to establish feeder system may be needed
Initial cost (million$/km)	1-8	10-30	15-30 at grade 30-75 elevated 60-180 underground	Varies widely, depending on infrastructure requirements
Typical capacity (passengers/hr/ direction/lane)	15,000 – 35,000	10,000 – 20,000	Up to 60,000	Up to 30,000
Operating speed (km/hr)	15-25 (higher for some commuter systems)	15-25	30-40	40+

Note: Passenger capacity and speed data also depend on the frequency of service, space between stations and extent of dedicated infrastructure (for buses). No comparisons that hold these factors constant were available.

As the table indicates, BRT systems can compete with rail systems in many respects, including movement of passengers per hour, and are much less expensive to build. While they usually do not match the passenger-carrying capacity of metros, cities can often afford to build a number of BRT lines for the price of one rail line. BRT systems can be built incrementally as funds allow, which is more difficult to do with rail systems. BRT systems also may have the advantage of flexibility – depending on design, some routes can be modified relatively easily after being built – while rail systems tend to be inflexible after completion.

On the other hand, implementing a BRT system may require taking road space away from other vehicles. But even if existing roadway space is given over to a BRT line, there is often an improvement in traffic flow, both from a reduction in the number of vehicles on the road and from removing buses that may have been slowing traffic when stopping to pick up passengers. Light rail systems may also require use of existing roadway space. Metros typically have little impact on existing roadway capacity and therefore may increase the overall capacity of the transport network substantially more than most bus systems. However, if one of the goals of adding a mass transit line is to encourage modal shifts away from personal vehicles, this may be encouraged by the removal of some roadway capacity.

Buses operating in general traffic are likely to perform much worse than those in busways and thus may not qualify as BRT systems even if they possess some of the other elements outlined above. The less buses are hindered by competition with other traffic for road space, the faster they can go and the more consistent service they can provide. In addition, dedicated roadway space can be designed to handle very large buses – with capacities of over 200 passengers for some articulated models. Such buses often cannot be used on normal shared roadway space due to difficulties at intersections and the large bus stop areas they require.

Allocating dedicated roadway infrastructure for bus systems can also make more room for bus stops, elevated platforms, and rapid bus boarding using multiple bus doors. In fact, several BRT systems use bus "stations" rather than bus stops, with fare payment occurring at the station entrance. This also speeds boarding. These features are an important part of the successful BRT systems in cities such as Curitiba and Bogota.

Whether or not dedicated roadway infrastructure is available, bus systems can benefit from a variety of technological and street design measures. These include traffic-signal prioritisation, better bus shelters, fewer stops, special ticketing systems, improved information systems for riders and potential riders and better pedestrian and bicycle access to stations. They can also benefit from the deployment of better buses, with features such as low-floor access (or raised platforms at floor level), larger capacity, more comfortable seating, smoother ride, and better acceleration.

Performance of Conventional Bus Systems

A primary reason for developing improved bus systems is the poor performance of conventional bus systems around the world over the past several decades. While buses have played a crucial role in moving people in urban areas, their share of passenger travel has declined in many cities, even those with quite low average incomes. This trend is shown for a number of cities in Tables 2.2 and 2.3.

Table 2.2 Modal Share of Passenger Travel
(percent)

	Year	Two and four wheelers	Bus	Taxi/ minibus	Train/ metro	Non-motor-ised	Total
Sao Paulo	1977	29	41		5	26	100
	1987	27	27		8	38	100
	1997	31	25		7	36	99
Mexico City	1986	25	42	11	22		100
	1995	22	8	56	14		100
Shanghai	1986	3	24			72	99
	1998	11	18			71	100
Dublin	1991	64	26		10		100
	1997	72	19		9		100

Note: Two and four wheelers combined due to data limitations for some cities; data for some modes not available or not applicable for some cities. Source: WBCSD, 2001 and IEA data.

Table 2.3 Changes Over Time in Daily Average Public Transport Trips in Selected Cities
(includes bus, rail and paratransit)

City	Year	Population (million)	Public Transport Trips/day	% of All Trips	Year	Population (million)	Public Transport Trips/day	% of All Trips
		Earlier Year				**Later Year**		
Hong Kong	1973	4.2	1.1	85	1992	5.6	1.7	89
Manila	1984	6.6	1.5	75	1996	9.6	1.5	78
Mexico	1984	17.0	0.9	80	1994	22.0	1.2	72
Moscow	1990	8.6	2.8	87	1997	8.6	2.8	83
Santiago	1977	4.1	1.0	70	1991	5.5	0.9	56
Sao Paolo	1977	10.3	1.0	46	1997	16.8	0.6	33
Seoul	1970	5.5	NA	67	1992	11.0	1.5	61
Shanghai	1986	13.0	0.4	24	1995	15.6	0.3	15
Warsaw	1987	1.6	1.3	80	1998	1.6	1.2	53

Source: WBCSD, 2001. NA = not available.

As shown in Table 2.2 (for bus systems) and Table 2.3 (for all transit systems, including paratransit[4]), the share of travel and trips by mass transit has declined in many cities. However, while the *share* has declined substantially, the travel levels by transit remain stable or continue to rise in many cities. In short, most of the growth in urban travel is occurring in private transport, especially two- and four-wheel vehicles.

The fact that transit systems have not kept up with private motorised transport is not surprising. Statistics show that there is a close correlation between growth in income and growth in ownership rates of private vehicles (first, two-wheelers in many countries, then four-wheel vehicles in nearly all countries). Given the comfort, convenience and flexibility of private vehicles, it might seem that there is little hope for cities to slow or reverse this trend, regardless of their investments in transit systems. But the experience of a few cities shows this is not true – transit can still thrive as cities mature and citizens become more wealthy. In cities like Hong Kong and Singapore, heavy investment in transit systems along with strict land-use policies and

---

4   Paratransit vehicles are relatively small (typically 8-24 seater) and often independently operated.

policies discouraging private vehicle use have helped maintain the market appeal of transit, despite high income levels. As can be seen in Table 2.3, in Hong Kong the share of trips taken by mass transit actually increased from 85% to 89% between 1973 and 1992. Examples of continuing high transit

Table 2.4 Transit System Problems and Potential Solutions using Bus Rapid Transit

Characteristic	Typical bus system (particularly in large developing cities)	Bus rapid transit system
Average bus speeds	Five to 15 km/hr depending on traffic, resulting in travel of 100-300 km per day	Twenty to 25 km/hr with travel of up to 500 km/day
Service frequency	Often 20 minute or longer wait time between buses	Typically 10 minutes or less between buses; more than 1 bus per minute on some Latin American routes at peak times
Passenger comfort	Overcrowded buses, poor seating, high temperatures in some cities	High capacity buses are generally well designed with better seating, easier boarding/alighting, sometimes air conditioned
Information on bus destinations, schedules	Routes and schedules often unclear, not adhered to	Frequent service reduces concern about schedule; real-time schedule display at bus stops is possible; improved route maps at bus stops; digital displays on board buses can provide real-time bus stop information
Urban area coverage, transfer	Bus routes often not well integrated, tickets not transferable to other buses; difficult to reach a wide range of locations within urban area	Complete system integration – often one ticket works for all buses within urban area. Co-ordination of service to reduce transfer times; paratransit routes can be converted to feeder routes for BRT trunk lines
Safety and aesthetics	Concerns regarding buses and stations are common, including safety and security; cleanliness; training and professionalism of staff	Usually provides substantial improvements in these areas. Off-bus ticket booths guarantee that waiting passengers are not completely alone

share can also be found in middle-income cities such as Curitiba and low-income cities like Bogota, where a similar emphasis has been placed on developing strong transit systems and adopting various supporting policies.

Transit systems are plagued by a number of characteristics that reduce their performance and attractiveness to potential riders. These are described in Table 2.4, along with potential solutions provided by BRT systems.

Examples of Bus Rapid Transit Systems around the World

The city of Curitiba, Brazil, has brought worldwide attention to the concept of BRT. The successes there have spawned hundreds of site visits by urban transit planners from around the world and myriad studies on the dos and don'ts of urban transit planning. Curitiba has an extensive commuter bus system that includes exclusive busways coupled with traffic signal prioritisation, tube-shaped fully-enclosed stations with level-floor boarding, advance fare collection and a number of other features designed to increase bus speeds and improve service. Several other comprehensive BRT systems based on the 'Curitiba model' have been developed or are under development – especially in Latin America. Several cities in North America have picked up on these concepts and are playing "catch-up", retrofitting advanced bus systems into sometimes quite sprawling metropolises. In Europe, many cities have developed well-integrated, if sometimes modest, versions of dedicated bus and bus-priority systems that fit well with their pedestrian-oriented urban centres. The following section reviews some of these programmes.

Curitiba and other Brazilian Cities

Curitiba's collective transportation system is built on a backbone of intersecting busways, supported by a large network of "feeder" buses. Development of the system was begun in the 1970s, with the aim of giving mass transit priority over small private vehicles. As of 2000, the Curitiba Integrated Transport Network operated 1,902 buses, making about 14,000 journeys daily, totalling 316,000 kilometres. About 1.9 million passengers are transported daily, similar to many metro systems. There is a reported 89% user satisfaction rate (Curitiba, 2001).

In Curitiba, buses running in busways account for over 70% of commute trips and nearly 50% of all daily motorised trips, with high average bus speeds and very high load factors (Gordon *et al*, 1999; Rabinowitch and Leitman, 1993). Dedicated "trunk lines" run along major avenues with up to three lanes accessible only to buses. Large double-articulated buses that can carry well over 200 passengers, relatively long distances between stations, and specially-designed "tube" stations for rapid boarding of passengers allow the system to deliver more "throughput" (passengers per hour past a given point) than many rail systems are able to achieve (Mereilles, 2000)[5].

Curitiba's system features "tube stations" and dedicated roadway infrastructure (courtesy Lloyd Wright, ITDP).

An important aspect of the bus transit system in Curitiba is its integrated tariff, which allows trips and transfers throughout the system for a single fare. It is estimated that around 80% of passengers use this benefit in their daily commute. In addition, while the flat tariff of about $0.65 is relatively high for Brazil, fare subsidies provided by businesses and directly by the government reduce the per-trip costs for those who need it.

The system is also integrated with eight other cities around Greater Curitiba via express BRT lanes. Throughout this system, fifty-eight kilometres of express bus lanes are complemented by 270 kilometres of feeder routes and 185 kilometres of interdistrict routes, serving about 65% of the metropolitan area.

Perhaps the most important aspect of the bus system in Curitiba is the manner in which it has been integrated with land-use development (and vice versa) over the past 30 years. High-density residential and commercial development has been permitted within walking distance of stations, with much lower densities elsewhere in the city. The close co-ordination with land use has served to maximise the efficiency of the system and to ensure that stations serve well-developed, relatively high-density areas (Meirelles, 2000).

Besides Curitiba, a number of other cities in Brazil have begun developing BRT systems, most featuring at least one busway corridor. These include Sao

---

5   Throughputs on Brazilian and other Latin American city busways often exceed 20,000 passengers per hour per direction.

Paulo (discussed in detail in Chapter 4), Belo Horizonte (capital of the state of Minas Gerais, population 2.2 million), Recife (capital of the state of Pernambuco, population 1.4 million), Porto Alegre (capital of Rio Grande do Sul, southern-most state of Brazil, population 1.3 million), Goiania (capital of the state of Goias, population 1.1 million), and Campinas (an important industrial and university centre, population 0.9 million).

Porto Alegre and Sao Paulo each have several busway corridors; the other cities each have one. All use a "trunk and feeder" system to ensure that travellers can easily get to the busway. Nearly all make extensive use of large capacity, articulated buses and the popular Latin-American feature of left-side doors to allow boarding from central stations located on the busway median.

Average passenger flows and load factors on the busways in Brazilian cities are very high, sometimes even exceeding the rated capacity of buses (Table 2.5). Flows in excess of 20,000 passengers per hour are routine, and flows reach 30,000 per hour in Sao Paulo. Few light-rail systems can match these numbers.

Table 2.5 Characteristics of Busways in Brazilian Cities

City	Busway location within city	Bus flows (average # of buses per hour, peak periods)	Bus capacity (seated plus standing)	Actual passenger flows	Average bus load factors
Belo Horizonte	Cristiano Machado	300	26,800	16,800	0.63
Campinas	Amoreiras	116	10,700	9,200	0.86
Curitiba	Eixo Sul	56	11,100	10,100	0.91
Goiania	Anhanguera	58	7,400	10,500	1.42
Porto Alegre	Farrapos	310	24,100	23,300	0.96
Recife	Caxanga	340	26,600	26,800	1.01
Sao Paulo	S. Amaro/ 9 de Julho	400	45,900	34,000	0.74

Source: Meirelles, 2000.

Other BRT Systems in Latin America

Elsewhere in Latin America, a number of large cities are aggressively developing BRT systems. Among the most notable are Bogota, Colombia and Quito, Ecuador.

In Bogota, the "TransMilenio" project envisions a city-wide system of rapid bus corridors by 2015. Operations started in 2000 and only three lines are in place so far, but they already carry more travellers than entire mass-transit systems in many other cities around the world: around 700,000 daily trips and up to 42,000 passengers per hour during peak times, with average bus speeds of 26 kilometres per hour. With a flat fare of 900 Colombian pesos (about $0.38), revenues are sufficient for the participating private bus companies to be profitable.

The citizens of Bogota, who so respect their system that they often dress up to ride on it, voted in 2000 to make the entire urban area car-free (except for taxis) during morning and evening peak periods – beginning in 2015, once most of the TransMilenio system is in place (Bogota project, 2000)[6]. One reason for this support is the existence of a well-publicised master plan that makes clear when and how the system will be expanded to all parts of the city. By 2015, 85% of the population will live within 500 metres of a TransMilenio station. A portion of the fuel tax in Bogota is dedicated to funding the capital costs of expanding the system (Penalosa, 2002).

Even weddings sometimes involve taking the TransMilenio (courtesy Oscar Diaz).

Another key to the success of this system is its ease of access for pedestrians. This includes integration with a pedestrian zone, and links with an expanding system of cycle-ways around the city. Secure parking for bicycles is provided at most stations. The city has also expanded the scope of "car-free Sundays", a long-standing tradition along the city's major corridors, to parts of the wider metropolitan area (Wright, 2002).

6   This vote was subsequently struck down by the Supreme court, but a new referendum is being considered.

Quito's "El Trolé" busway system has been developed using electric trolley buses in exclusive lanes, with several trolley routes feeding into the main corridor. Terminals on both ends of the route are served by a large number of feeder routes. The system uses raised platforms and prepaid ticketing to ensure convenient and rapid boarding. Good facilities are in place for pedestrian and bicycle access to the system. Since the introduction of the system, bus ridership in Quito has risen significantly. The electric buses are powered from overhead lines and although this costs more than some other bus options, the El Trolé system produces no urban emissions. Nor does it produce any greenhouse emissions, since the electricity is produced mainly by hydropower.

The dramatic improvements in bus systems in Bogota and Quito have begun to spur the development of BRT systems in other cities in the region. For example, Cuenca, Ecuador, has recently developed a detailed plan for its BRT. Cuenca started by formalising its previously unregulated bus operators, removing many of its oldest buses from service, implementing an innovative parking scheme and upgrading pedestrian services (ITDP, 2001).

BRT Systems in North America

Despite having the highest car-ownership levels in the world, a number of North American cities have begun to develop busway systems, and several have made considerable progress.

Ottawa probably has the most comprehensive busway system in North America. Its "Transitway" was built in stages from 1978 through 1996 and features a 31-kilometre bus-only corridor leading to the central business district, where it connects to exclusive bus lanes on city streets (FTA, 2001). Over 75% of passenger bus trips are made using the Transitway. It was constructed largely on rail rights-of-way and was designed for possible conversion to rail should ridership warrant. The main Transitway routes use articulated buses with "proof-of-prepayment" fare collection to speed boarding – only one quarter of the riders pay cash. Feeder buses operate on a timed transfer schedule. Ridership and average load factors on this system are much higher than on most bus systems in other cities. Like Curitiba, an important aspect of the busway system in Ottawa is careful co-ordination with the urban-planning and development programme. Ottawa's planning rules and guidelines strongly promote transit-oriented development, both in terms of location and in terms of providing infrastructure (e.g. sidewalks, bike facilities) that complement the transit system (FTA, 2002).

According to the US General Accounting Office (GAO, 2001), at least 17 cities in the US are developing or planning to develop BRT-style systems. GAO analysis of capital costs for the development of BRT systems using busways or HOV lanes (Table 2.6), indicates that the average cost is about one-quarter to one-half as much as for light rail systems. Systems relying on dedicated lanes on arterial streets are only about one-fiftieth the cost to implement.

Table 2.6 Capital Costs for BRT and Light-rail Projects in the United States

	Number of facilities examined	Capital cost ($ millions) per kilometre		
		Average	Lowest	Highest
Bus rapid transit				
Busways	9	8.4	4.3	34.1
HOV	8	5.6	1.1	23.3
Arterial streets	3	0.4	0.1	6.0
Light rail	18	21.6	7.7	73.7

Source: GAO, 2001.

Of the US BRT systems, Pittsburgh's may be the most developed, with three busways heading south, west and east out of the central business district, all on exclusive rights-of-way. Pittsburgh's busways feature extensive park-and-ride facilities and biking trails along some sections. Among other US cities that have begun to develop BRT systems are Eugene Oregon, Orlando Florida, and Cleveland Ohio.

Even some of the most car-oriented US cities have begun to develop BRT systems. In Los Angeles, a recent initiative called "Rapidbus" aims to dramatically improve bus service by giving buses priority in traffic, particularly at intersections. An initial Rapidbus route runs along the 40 kilometre Wilshire-Whittier corridor. Buses have priority at intersections, which offer an "advanced green" or "delayed green" signal to reduce bus waiting time at red lights. New bus stops were also built along this route, using a GPS system and real-time electronic displays to indicate the waiting time until the next bus. While there are no dedicated lanes, this approach has raised bus speeds an average of 15%, increased ridership significantly and lowered fuel use slightly (LA, 2001). This type of signal-priority system for buses is well known in Sweden, where many cities have employed it for years.

Bus Systems in Europe

Few, if any, European cities have Curitiba-style busway systems with entire corridors dedicated to buses. However, many cities have buses or tramways that operate on dedicated lanes. For example, Paris recently nearly doubled the total kilometres of bus/taxi lanes in the city. Many European cities have adopted advanced systems, such as global-positioning system (GPS) based tracking systems that allow real-time bus arrival information to be displayed at bus stops (see section on bus system technologies, below). Amsterdam combines a complex web of bus/taxi-only lanes with bicycle lanes that makes the city extremely easy to get around in – except, perhaps, for those travelling by private automobile.

In many European cities, surface mass transit is so well integrated with the urban area and land-use patterns that "bus rapid transit" is not really applicable or needed. For example, in Zurich the average resident makes about 1.6 transit trips per day – one of the highest rates in the world – even though there is no underground metro system (Kenworthy and Laube, 1999). Over the past few decades, Zurich has built a system of pedestrian streets, tramways, bus lanes and bicycle-friendly terrain. Frequent transit users pay very low fares. Cars are relegated to a relatively minor role, with many restrictions on where they may travel and park. As a result, many trips are faster via bike or public transit than by car (Cervero, 1998). Though no Ottawa- or Curitiba-style busways exist in Zurich, many technologies to make buses more attractive are employed. These include bus tracking systems and real-time schedule information for passengers, bus priority at intersections, smart fare card technology and integration of fares to make transfers throughout the city easy and cheap.

Many other cities in Europe are similar to Zurich in their zest for favouring public transit and creating a friendly environment for non-motorised vehicles.

Cities like Amsterdam, Copenhagen, Munich and Vienna are well known for this, but many other cities do as well or better in terms of the average number of trips per person, per day, via public transit and on non-motorised modes.

One important question for many European cities is whether to continue to build tramways – roadway-based rail systems with vehicles that are typically electric – or shift to more bus-oriented systems. While electric trams produce no (direct) air pollution, and are generally popular, tram systems are also typically much more expensive to develop than bus systems, and more difficult to modify once installed (Henscher, 1999). Given the relatively low cost and the flexibility of bus systems, plus the fact that very clean internal combustion engine buses are now available (as discussed in Chapter 3), the case for building tramway systems is not as strong as it once was.

IMPROVING BUS SYSTEMS: POTENTIAL BENEFITS

Decisions to improve transit systems should be based, at least in part, on an estimate of the likely resulting social benefits, such as reductions in emissions, fuel use, and traffic. So should decisions about *how* to make improvements: should major system upgrades be made or should the priority be to upgrade to better buses with investments in propulsion technology and clean fuels? But estimating the relative impacts of different options is not easy. This section explores this question by presenting scenarios that indicate under what circumstances it may be appropriate to focus on different objectives.

The scenarios presented below focus primarily on the choice between adding bus capacity using standard, relatively low-technology buses v. replacing existing buses with cleaner ones. The results suggest the following: when there is scope for attracting significant numbers of riders who would otherwise travel by smaller motor vehicles, then the social benefits of expanding bus capacity are likely to be substantial – in terms of net reductions in fuel use, pollutant and CO_2 emissions and use of road space. This appears to be true even if relatively low-cost, "standard" diesel buses are used that produce fairly high pollutant emissions compared to more advanced buses.

However, there are other situations – if expected bus ridership is low or if new riders are being attracted primarily from non-motorised modes – where expanding capacity by adding standard buses may provide few benefits, at least in terms of emissions and fuel use. In such cases it may make more sense to give priority to replacing existing buses with cleaner ones.

Many large developing cities appear likely to fall into the first category, where improving transit (and especially developing BRT systems) offers the chance to dramatically increase ridership and provide substantial reductions in fuel use, emissions and road-space requirements. It is clear that in cities like Curitiba and Bogota, the ridership impacts of developing their BRT systems are large. As we demonstrate below, the primary benefits of BRT systems – or of any expansion of transit systems where buses run reasonably full – are likely to be due more to mode shifting than the particular fuels or propulsion technologies used by buses.

Impacts of Expanding Bus System Capacity

Improving a bus system, or even expanding the capacity of an existing system by adding buses, carries with it a number of potential short- and long-term impacts. Increasing capacity can immediately spur mode-switching as more seats become available and service improves (for example, buses become more frequent). Upgrading to cleaner buses can immediately reduce bus emissions and fuel use. In the longer run an improved bus system can have an impact on land use and overall travel demand. These different impacts are elaborated below:

■ **Short-run impacts from an increase in bus capacity.** Increasing bus system capacity will attract some riders immediately, in particular those who did not previously have good access to bus service. This creates immediate impacts in terms of emissions, energy use and road space as new riders abandon other modes and other vehicles are used less. In a case where many buses are added, or a large increase in system capacity is provided by implementing a BRT system, a significant number of other vehicles may no longer be needed at all. Over time, this increase in bus capacity may avoid the addition of many other new vehicles to the roads.

■ **Short-run impacts of technology substitution.** As discussed in Chapter 3, there can be significant short-run benefits from the introduction of cleaner buses. For example, a Euro-II-compliant diesel bus could be bought instead of a standard ("Euro-0") diesel or a reconditioned second-hand bus. The direct impacts of the technology change on emissions and fuel use are measurable. But the substitution of one technology for another can also have mode switching impacts. For example, a modern low-floor bus may be more attractive to certain types of riders. On the other hand, if running more expensive buses spurs a fare increase, some riders may choose to switch away from buses to another type of vehicle. The potential for this type of secondary impact from technology improvements should not be ignored.

- **Long-run impacts.** Over time, expanding bus system capacities and developing better systems could affect where people choose to live and work – and the way land is developed. A high-speed bus service, with stops every half- kilometre, could spur development close to those stops. This is more likely when planners implement zoning and other policies that encourage development around bus stations. If a "critical mass" of bus routes in a city is improved and expanded, they may shape the entire land use and growth patterns of the city. Cities like Curitiba and Ottawa are examples of this.

Although the longer-term impacts are difficult to quantify, it is possible to get some indication of the shorter-term impacts of improving buses and bus systems. A key assumption in our analysis is that as buses are added, or systems are improved and expanded, riders are drawn away from other modes. The numbers of riders attracted, and types of modes they are drawn from, determine the mode-switching impacts of the changes to the bus system. Since in many cities bus ridership is declining, actions taken to strengthen bus systems can have strong positive impacts simply by preventing further shifts away from buses. The better, and larger, the bus system, the less likely it is that riders will abandon them for other modes. Our analysis can be applied in this situation as well.

To simplify our analysis, we focus on "adding one bus". This can have a variety of mode-switching impacts. The worst outcome is that the bus attracts no riders and thus simply adds one more large, polluting vehicle to the road. Perhaps the best scenario is a full bus that attracts only former drivers of single-occupant cars, highly polluting motorcycles and small paratransit vehicles. These two cases represent ends of the spectrum and most circumstances fall somewhere in the middle. But in many large cities in developing countries, something close to the "best case" may regularly occur. Buses tend to run full (or overloaded) a high percentage of the time. And individuals taking the bus may commonly be foregoing other motorised options. For example, in Dhaka, Bangladesh, a "premium bus service" is provided to commuters from certain suburban neighbourhoods who do, in many instances, own cars, but prefer taking the bus to work[7]. Similarly, in Delhi, a survey of riders of commuter buses indicated that nearly half own two-wheelers (motorcycles or scooters) and 10% to 15% own cars[8].

The following two scenarios use different assumptions regarding the number of riders-per-bus that a capacity-expansion programme might attract, and which modes these riders might switch from. The two scenarios can be considered 'optimistic' and 'pessimistic'. The scenarios also estimate the incremental impacts of upgrading from a standard new bus to cleaner buses. To provide some sense of real-world vehicle characteristics, vehicle-emissions estimates for Delhi are used. As mentioned, the results are presented in terms of adding or upgrading one bus.

Scenario I

The first scenario assumes that an additional bus is placed in service with 120 passenger capacity. This bus operates at half capacity, carrying an average of 60 passengers over the course of a normal day. These passengers are assumed to be drawn from a variety of travel modes, as shown in Figure 2.1.

Since these riders are drawn from other modes, a certain number of other vehicles are displaced, i.e. do not make the trip they would otherwise have made. In order to know how many other vehicles are displaced, it is necessary to make assumptions regarding how many passengers each mode typically carries. These assumptions are presented in Table 2.7. This table also provides estimates of the road space taken by each vehicle type.

By combining the assumptions in Table 2.7 with the mode-switching assumptions in Figure 2.1, impacts on road-space requirements can be estimated (Table 2.8).

---

7   Personal communication, Abdul Alam Bhuiyan, Bangladesh Transport Foundation.
8   Personal communication, Dinesh Mohan (IIT, Delhi).

Figure 2.1 Scenario I: Former Travel Modes of Passengers Switching to a Bus Added to the System

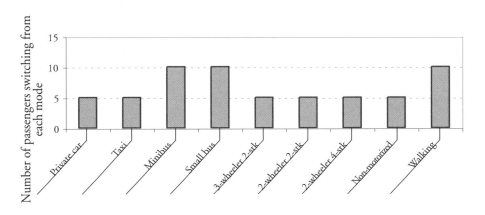

Note: Total of 60 passengers; 2-stk is two-stroke engine, 4-stk is four-stroke engine (less polluting than a two-stroke).

Table 2.7 Vehicle Capacity, Load and Road-space Assumptions

	Vehicle passenger capacity	Average passenger load per vehicle	Road space required (in units of one bus-equivalent)
Full-size bus (any type)	120	60 (in this scenario)	1.0
Private car	5	1.5	0.5
Taxi	3	1.2	0.5
Minibus / paratransit	15	12	0.65
Small diesel bus	40	30	0.8
3-wheeler 2-stroke	3	1.5	0.33
2-wheeler 2-stroke	2	1.2	0.25
2-wheeler 4-stroke	2	1.2	0.25
Non-motorised mode	3	1.5	0.25
Walking	1	1	0

Note: the specific road space requirements of each vehicle type vary and are dependent on vehicle speed. This table represents a rough average across different driving situations.

Table 2.8 Scenario I: Mode-switching Impacts of One Bus

	Riders switching from each mode	Riders per vehicle for that mode (average)	Total number of displaced vehicles	Road space freed up (bus-equivalent)
Private car	5	1.5	3.3	1.7
Taxi (older car)	5	1.2	4.2	2.1
Minibus / paratransit	10	12	0.8	0.5
Small diesel bus	10	30	0.2	0.2
3-wheeler, 2-stroke engine	5	1.5	3.3	1.1
2-wheeler, 2-stroke engine	5	1.2	4.2	1.0
2-wheeler, 4-stroke engine	5	1.2	4.2	1.0
Non-motorised mode	5	1.5	3.3	0.8
Walking	10	0	0.0	0.0
Total	60		23.5	8.4

In this scenario, the space-equivalent of eight buses is removed from the road for each actual bus added. Fuel efficiency and emissions impacts of adding this bus can also be estimated. The following assumptions (Table 2.9) were used for different types of buses as well as for other vehicles. The bus emissions data is derived from the "Euro" system of emissions standards (discussed in Chapter 3), and estimates for other vehicles are based on data from South Asia, such as Delhi and Dhaka.

Given all of these assumptions, the following sets of impacts were estimated for Scenario 1 (Figures 2.2a and 2.2b).

Table 2.9 Assumptions for Vehicle Efficiency and Emissions Factors

	Fuel use (L/100km)	HC (g/km)	CO (g/km)	NO$_x$ (g/km)	PM (g/km)
"Standard" (Euro 0) diesel bus	50	2.1	12.7	10.0	2.0
Euro II bus	50	0.5	2.0	10.0	0.5
Euro IV bus	50	0.1	0.5	2.0	0.2
Zero emissions bus	40	0.0	0.0	0.0	0.0
Private car	9	1.5	9.5	1.9	0.2
Taxi (older car)	9	6.2	28.9	2.7	0.3
Minibus / paratransit	20	0.7	5.4	2.5	0.9
Small Diesel Bus	30	2.1	12.7	10.0	2.0
3-wheeler, 2-stroke engine	5	7.7	12.3	0.1	0.5
2-wheeler, 2-stroke engine	3.5	5.2	8.3	0.1	0.5
2-wheeler, 4-stroke engine	3	0.7	8.3	0.4	0.1
Non-motorised mode	0	0.0	0.0	0.0	0.0

Source: IEA data, mostly based on estimates made for Delhi and Dhaka by Xie et al, 1998 and 1998b.

Figure 2.2 Estimated Reductions in Road-space Requirement, Fuel Use and Emissions from the Introduction of One Additional Bus

2.2a: Measured as the number of "bus-equivalents" of reduction

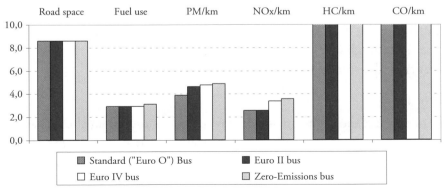

Note: For HC/km and CO/km, reductions are well above 10 times the emissions of one bus, because diesel buses emit very low levels of these pollutants compared to two and three-wheelers.

2.2b: Measured as a percentage reduction in total impacts

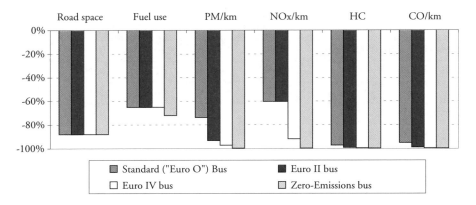

Note: The percentage reduction includes reductions from displacement of vehicles minus new impacts from the added bus.

The above figures indicate that in this scenario, adding one bus results in substantial reductions in the use of road space, fuel use, and emissions of each of the four listed pollutants. For some factors, such as road space, the reductions are many times the impact caused by the bus itself.

This analysis also sheds some light on the relative benefits of switching to cleaner buses. Certainly, a cleaner bus will yield lower emissions, but in this scenario the emissions reductions from technology choice are overshadowed by reductions from mode switching (and the resulting "subtraction" of other vehicles)[9]. With the exception of NO_x, the impact of upgrading to cleaner buses is minor, regardless of whether the improvement is to a clean (Euro II) bus, a very clean (Euro IV) bus or a zero-emission bus. Dramatic reductions in road space, fuel use, and most emissions can be achieved through displacing other vehicles with any bus, even the "Euro 0" buses typically sold in the developing world.

Scenario II

In our second, more pessimistic scenario, it is assumed that the bus added to the system carries only half as many passengers, on average, as in Scenario 1 (30 riders instead of 60). It is also assumed that most of these passengers

---

9   This scenario assumes that a basic bus can attract as many riders as a cleaner bus. For all four bus types shown in the figures above, an average of 60 riders is assumed (half of "crush" occupancy). This is actually much lower than averages on most Latin-American BRT systems.

switch from smaller buses and paratransit vehicles, and that none comes from automobiles or two-wheelers (Figure 2.3).

Figure 2.3 Scenario II: Former Travel Modes of Passengers Switching to a Bus Added to the System

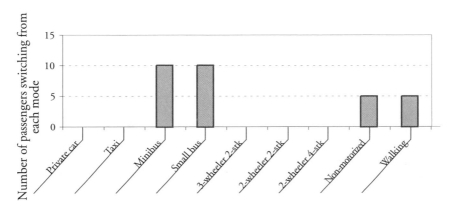

Apart from the much lower ridership and different mode-switching patterns, this scenario matches the first scenario in terms of assumed average vehicle load factors, fuel efficiency and emissions factors for each mode type.

The effects of these different mode-switching assumptions on the outcome, by bus type, are shown in Figures 2.4a and 2.4b. In this scenario, a "standard" bus provides far fewer benefits than in Scenario 1. In fact the only real net benefit it provides is a reduction in the use of road space, formerly required by small buses and paratransit vehicles to carry the 30 passengers. Due to the space-efficiency of the large bus, even running at one-quarter full it cuts the required road space by nearly half (note from the figure that it eliminates about 1.6 other bus-equivalents, but it adds 1 bus, so the net reduction is only 0.6 bus-equivalents). Since the bus only displaces a few smaller vehicles, and is a high emitter itself, the result is actually a net increase in fuel use and emissions.

On the other hand, upgrading to cleaner buses now provides much larger incremental benefits over a "basic" bus, and is critical in order to obtain net emissions reductions. For example, a Euro-II bus provides around 50% reductions for HC, CO and PM. A Euro-IV bus, with its much greater NO_x reductions, is needed in order to get a net NO_x reduction. For all of the different bus types, there is an estimated increase in fuel consumption relative to the displaced vehicles, although there could still be a reduction in *petroleum* use if the new bus is alternative-fuelled.

Figure 2.4 Estimated Reductions in Pollutants and Other Impacts from the Introduction of One Additional Bus

2.4a: Measured as the number of "bus-equivalents" of reduction

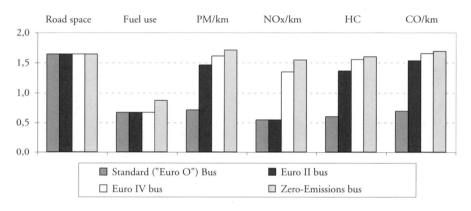

Note: One bus-equivalent of reduction is needed just to off-set the impact of each standard bus.

2.4b: Measured as a percentage reduction in total impacts

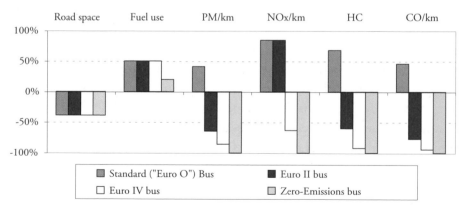

Many other scenarios are possible, including some that are more optimor pessimistic than these. The primary point here is to demonstrate that when ridership is fairly high and is drawn largely from paratransit and private motor vehicles, it is not necessary to use "clean" or advanced technology buses to achieve large social benefits. Under other circumstances (lower ridership levels and relatively few riders drawn from small private vehicles), buses may not provide many emissions or fuel use benefits unless they are clean, low-emitting and efficient.

For those cities that have a reasonable expectation of high ridership on an expanded bus system, and are interested in maximising social benefits, expanding the system probably should take precedence over upgrading individual buses. However, once an improved bus system is in place, technology improvements may be the only way to continue to gain emissions reductions and fuel savings. Obviously, if these two approaches can be undertaken concurrently, this may be the best strategy to rapidly achieve maximum benefits.

NEW TECHNOLOGIES FOR BUS SYSTEMS

A number of emerging technologies are available to enhance bus service, even for cases where buses must continue to share the road with other vehicles. Three of the most important technologies are described here.

Traffic Signal Priority Systems

Buses can be given a very apparent boost relative to other vehicles by providing them with signal priority at intersections. Through relatively simple technical means, signals can be set to detect the approach of a qualifying bus and either hold the green signal for longer than normal or advance the green in order to let buses start early. Where buses have a dedicated lane the signal can even be set to show a special "bus-only" green.

In one type of system, each bus carries an emitter which sends an encoded message to a detector mounted near the traffic signal as the bus approaches the intersection. The detector then sends a signal to override the normal operation of the signal control system. If the signal is already green, the phase selector tells the controller to hold the green until the bus passes. Once the bus passes through the intersection, the system returns the signal to normal operation. The signal priority system can also be linked with a communication network that also tracks bus location and provides information to passengers.

Priority signalisation generally cannot eliminate signal delays for buses entirely, since such an aggressive override system would cause intolerable disruption to other traffic, especially cross traffic. In most cities that currently employ a signal priority system, the normal signal cycle can only be overridden for five or ten seconds. In some cases, only buses running behind schedule are provided with advance greens, such as in Vancouver, Canada (FTA, 2002b). Still, signal priority systems reduce signal delays for buses by up to 50% and improve average bus speeds by anywhere from 10% to 30%.

The cost to implement a simple system for providing bus priority in developing countries can be quite low, only a few thousand dollars per intersection. More complex systems, involving central tracking and control of buses, such as in Los Angeles, cost more – but the payback times are short. Taking into account faster bus travel and reduced idle time at red lights, the payback time for the LA system, covering 222 intersections, has been estimated to be about 18 months, with a benefit/cost ratio of 6:1 over the expected ten-year life of the system (LA, 2001).

Bus Tracking and Passenger Information Systems

Systems to track the location of buses on a real-time basis, typically employing global positioning systems (GPS), are increasingly being used to improve the spacing of buses and ensure they are running on time. Additionally, they can provide passengers with real-time information such as the expected arrival time of the next few buses. These systems greatly improve the reliability and overall performance of bus systems, and have been shown to increase both rider satisfaction and ridership. (Ristola, 2000).

Elements of bus tracking systems can include:

- **Interactive Terminals** located at bus stops to help passengers plan their journeys and find out about arrival and departure times.

- **Electronic displays** at bus stops that give passengers real-time arrival information about the next few buses, reducing uncertainty and perhaps enabling some last-minute shopping without fear of missing the bus.

- **Information displays on buses** that remind passengers of approaching stops or indicate connections to other bus lines. Real-time, on-board information can decrease the stress of finding a stop, especially for passengers unfamiliar with the route.

- **Information available over the internet** that can be accessed at home or office, or even by cell phone, and can include information about routes, fares, schedules, traffic delays, and even expected bus arrival times at nearby stops.

Typical systems use a satellite-based global positioning system (GPS) as the centrepiece for bus-tracking and passenger information systems. These systems may comprise on-board computers in each bus that continuously track the position of the vehicle based on the GPS signal, adjusted by odometer readings and stop time. The bus route is also typically recorded in the system, requiring each driver to enter a tracking number when starting the bus in the morning. This information is then fed to a central computer that can automatically provide various information to bus stops or the internet. The information can also be used as part of a traffic signal priority system to identify tardy buses and help them get back on schedule.

While the costs to develop a bus information and control system can be quite variable, depending on the size of the system and components included, a fairly large system with many of the key components may cost under $5000 per bus. The cost for some needed equipment, such as GPS receivers for buses, has fallen considerably in recent years.

Bus Ticketing Systems

In many cities in the developing world, bus operators have one or two people to manually collect fares on each bus. While in some systems this may be the most cost-effective or most reliable way to collect fares, in others it may make sense to automate fare collection, or at least move it off the bus. Automated fare collection has two main advantages: it can reduce bus boarding times and it can increase the reliability and convenience of fare collection. In addition, automation can facilitate the use of a single ticket throughout the system, although this also depends on the development of a single revenue network, which may be a major step in cities with many competing bus operators.

Ticketing that is done off-bus, for example in bus stations, can allow much more rapid boarding and can increase average bus speeds (and reduce passenger travel times) significantly. In advanced systems such as those used in Bogota and Curitiba, where buses are equipped with three or more doors and raised floors that match platform heights, passengers typically enter and exit the bus within a few seconds, compared to 30 seconds or longer in systems that require boarding through a single door.

A bus-station-based ticket system usually requires that the bus station be physically separated from the surrounding area, with turnstile access to a boarding area, and at least one person stationed at the stop to sell tickets, make change and monitor entry. The presence of a ticket-taker can have the positive side effect of increasing security around the bus station and – just as importantly – increasing the sense of safety for travellers after dark or when there are not many others waiting for a bus.

Quito's BRT features a pre-boarding fare card system (courtesy Lloyd Wright, ITDP).

Automated ticketing may reduce the need for on-board ticket takers, but it may provide an even bigger benefit in terms of reduced single-ticket purchases. Tickets that can hold value for multiple journeys, such as weekly or monthly passes, can dramatically reduce the frequency purchases undertaken by each regular rider. The opportunities for using this approach have expanded with the development of "smart cards", using electronic chips or magnetic strips to store value. As passengers enter a station or board a bus, a card-reading machine determines the card's value and debits the appropriate amount. There are two types of card readers: "contact" readers that require physical contact with a card and "proximity" readers that can read cards held a few inches away. Systems under development will be able to read cards carried in passengers' pockets or purses. (FTA, 2001).

Smart cards used for rapid entry directly onto buses, especially multi-door buses, create the risk of high incidences of illegal travel if the doors are unmonitored. In some cases, random checking of passengers may be sufficient to prevent this problem. The metro system in Paris (RATP) relies on this approach.

Smart cards can be programmed for time or distance-based pricing by recording when and where a passenger enters a transit system and debiting the appropriate amount from the card balance according to the exit point, regardless of the number of transfers made during the trip.

Advanced smart-card systems are currently fairly expensive, largely due to the cost of the cards themselves. They currently cost up to $5 each to produce, but the cost is dropping (Ventura County, 2001). As the industry grows, expanded production is expected to bring the production costs below $1 per card (FTA, 2001). In poorer countries the cost may need to drop still further in order to be cost-effective for bus systems, although smart cards are already in use in Bogota, with a per-capita annual income of about $2,000.

IMPROVING BUS SYSTEM MANAGEMENT

In many developing cities, most buses are operated by independent bus companies or have been partially privatised. In some cities private companies have grown up to fill vacuums created by inadequate service of the public bus systems. Often many small, independent bus providers survive on a day-to-day basis. These companies are not able to make major investments in buses or bus systems. Some consolidation of bus service is probably needed in such cities to improve service and increase purchasing power for investment in new bus systems and technologies.

The problem of small-scale, fly-by-night operators is endemic in many bus systems around the world, leading to poor performance and low ridership (usually in the form of low numbers of overfull buses). Much of the problem can be traced to the manner in which the bus system is regulated, licensed and managed. Deficiencies in these areas can lead to a chaotic situation where intense competition, almost literally for each passenger, relegates strategic planning, investment and co-ordinated service to the "back of the bus".

Some cities provide outstanding transit service by operating it themselves. Others have successfully licensed all or part of it to private businesses. Innovative approaches include having different companies contract to handle different bus-related services. For example, in Bogota bus companies are paid per bus-kilometre of service provided, while fares are collected at stations by a separate company.

Well-designed regulations also play a key role. The private sector is able to provide very efficient, responsive bus services at affordable fares – when operators have incentives to meet users' needs. These incentives derive from the regulatory system, particularly the nature of licensing procedures and contracts. Competition is the most effective incentive; the risk of losing the right to provide service to another company tends to be the key ingredient in encouraging high quality service.

When competition extends down to the level of bus-versus-bus, the usual result is very poor service and sometimes a complete breakdown of the system.

Problems Associated with Excessive Competition

In many cities, regulators licence each bus to operate on a specific route. These regulations do not specify the service level for the overall route, so different buses serving the same route might not work together to provide co-ordinated service. Instead, buses compete with each other for passengers, behaving more like taxis than buses. Some of the problems resulting from this practice include:

■ Bus companies often sub-lease their buses to drivers, ensuring that payment is made for use of the bus (rather than employing drivers and risking that fares will not be fully transferred by drivers to the company). This reinforces the tendency of drivers to act independently.

■ Bus stops are often infrequently and not properly used; buses tend to stop anywhere to pick up a passenger. "Wave downs" often block traffic and slow travel speeds. Or multiple buses may stop concurrently at a crowded bus stop, clogging the street and slowing traffic.

■ Many cities rely heavily on bus terminals as changing points for passengers. This is considered efficient since passengers can choose from many different bus routes at a terminal. But the terminal system in many cities is plagued with problems and inefficiencies, such as high terminal entry fees for buses and long waiting periods as each bus idles until it is full before leaving. Conditions for travellers are often unsafe and unhealthy. The need for terminals may be overrated; they are not an important part of some of the most successful bus systems. For terminals to work, a high degree of co-ordination is needed between different routes and bus companies in order to manage bus arrivals and departures efficiently.

Creating Competition that Works

There are a number of different approaches to competition for bus systems. In its recent transport review, the World Bank (2001) provides a spectrum of possible regulatory arrangements, ranging from pure competition to complete government control and operation of the system. Some of the different approaches are summarised below:

Gross Cost Service Contracting involves contracting with a private bus operator for specified services at a fixed price, or one based on one or more parameters of service such as vehicle kilometres. The contract is usually awarded through competitive tendering. The operator must pass through all fare revenues, or revenues can be collected separately. This approach removes most of the problems associated with excessive competition, but oversight is necessary to ensure that the operator provides the specified service. In Bogota, which uses this approach, buses are tracked using a GPS system. Vehicle kilometres – the basis for payment – are independently verified.

Net Cost Service Contracting is similar in some respects to gross cost contracting, but requires the operator to derive revenues from fares. This increases operator risk since the revenues may vary unpredictably, and may make it difficult to co-ordinate service between different providers or to have a common fare system. However, it avoids the need for complex fare collection systems and security arrangements.

Franchising involves giving the operator nearly full responsibility for managing the operation of the bus system, within agreed parameters. Operational assets may still be owned by the city authority, but the operator typically handles all procurement and maintenance and is more involved in overall management of the system. Depending on fare and ridership levels, it may be difficult for franchises to make a profit and some subsidisation may be needed.

Concession takes the next step beyond franchising and entails an exclusive right to provide a service in a designated area, usually without any payment in either direction between the city authority and the operator. Contracts are typically long-term in order to provide the operator time and incentive to invest in the system and build up business. Maximum fares or minimum levels of service may be required by the authority.

Regardless of the level of competition or the type of contract, certain general conditions appear necessary for effective competition in the bus sector. Meakin (2001) identifies four such conditions: a supportive government policy, clear transport objectives, a legal framework enabling fair competition, and institutional capacity to promote, direct, and regulate competition.

An important feature of "competition that works" is a well-designed and executed tendering process. The tendering process creates a competition for the right to provide bus services in a specific area or on a specific route. The process must allocate routes fairly and objectively. It should be done publicly and transparently. Meakin identifies four key criteria in evaluating tender bids:

- Proposed fares and fare structure.

- Level of service: frequency, regularity, capacity, daily operating period.

- Quality of service: bus capacity, specification, age, condition, required equipment, safety considerations.

- Environmental impact: emissions standards and fuel type.

The task of the regulator is to guide the development of the bus sector, manage the tender process, monitor operators' performance, and ensure that minimum vehicle and service levels are respected and that competition is fair and equal. It is also important that operators not be over-regulated to the point where they are unable to operate profitably when they provide quality service. For example, excessive restrictions on fares can undermine the ability of operators to provide adequate service. Studies of willingness to pay, even in very poor cities, suggest that people are often willing to pay a higher fare for improved service.

HOW TO AFFORD BETTER BUSES

A transit agency, whether municipally-owned or privatised, confronts many of the same "bottom-line" questions as any business: will revenues exceed costs this year? Are profits sufficient for new investment? Will high front-end investments yield payoffs in future years? Unlike purely private enterprises, however, transit agencies are often responsible to public interests, where investments may be guided by a mandate to deliver an equitable public service, to account for public externalities (pollution), or to provide for future generations (e.g. sustainability). Thus, transit agencies are challenged to make investment decisions that both balance the books and meet public service requirements.

One thing is clear: increasing bus speeds is very important for increasing revenues, balancing the books and being able to afford better buses. Slow bus speeds reduce the total kilometres that a bus can travel each day, and therefore the number of passengers that board – in turn lowering the revenues that the bus generates.

Faster-moving buses, with shorter waiting times and more reliable service, are the keys to increasing ridership. In cities with bad traffic and low average speeds for all vehicles, getting buses moving can give them a clear edge over other forms of travel.

Table 2.10 indicates that the impacts of different bus speeds and ridership levels on bus revenue can be large. It provides indicative data for a city like Delhi. A comparison is also shown with a "typical" bus in an OECD country[10]. The revealing statistic is not that revenue generated by a bus in South Asia is lower than in the OECD, which is not surprising since fares are much lower. It is that revenue could be tripled without changing fares, by increasing bus speeds and increasing the average number of passengers on each bus.

Table 2.10 Indicative Bus Operating Characteristics and Revenues for Buses in South Asia and OECD

	South Asia Current	South Asia Improved	OECD Current
Fare (US$)	$0.10	$0.10	$1.00
Average number of riders	40	60	25
Average boardings/km	10	15	5
Average speed (km/hr)	8	16	16
Distance (km/day)	150	300	300
Daily revenues per bus	$150	$450	$1,500
Annual revenues per bus	$54,000	$162,000	$540,000

Note: assumptions for fare, average ridership and speed are indicative and used to illustrate the differences.

10   Values, of course, vary considerably and data on the actual averages are poor.

With limited revenues to pay for better buses, many cities and bus companies are stuck with older, poorly maintained buses. These buses feature little or no pollution control; they are typically outdated vehicles, in many cases converted from truck frames or bought second-hand from developed countries. Poor fuel quality – in the form of high-sulphur diesel fuel – combined with poor engines make buses in the developing world major sources of particulate matter and NO_x emissions, and therefore of ozone (smog) as well. Buses are often seen as a major part of the problem rather than part of the solution.

Budgets for upgrading buses or replacing them, or even replacing worn parts, can be tiny or non-existent. While cities around the world often provide subsidies to transit systems, financial pressures and competing obligations often make it difficult to preserve existing subsidies, not to mention increase them. In many cities, bus operators will need to generate their own revenues in order to afford better buses.

With very low bus fares prevalent in South Asia and elsewhere in the developing world, bus speeds below 10 kilometres per hour are simply too low to recover the costs of new, clean buses that provide comfortable, reliable service. In South Asia, a medium-size bus that can carry 60-80 passengers costs about $35,000. A similar-sized, modern OECD-style bus costs $75,000 or more. To recover the capital and maintenance costs of such a bus, revenues per bus probably need to double. Increased revenues could be achieved in four ways: by increasing fares, increasing load factors, increasing speeds and daily travel distances, and by other activities such as putting advertising on buses. It may be possible to raise fares somewhat in some places, especially if the quality of service improves. But increasing fares could also push riders onto other modes — hence any changes must be considered carefully. It is in the areas of bus capacity, speed and service that the greatest gains can be made, with the biggest impacts for affording better buses.

3

BUS TECHNOLOGIES AND FUELS

A range of engine technologies is available to improve bus performance and better bus designs exist that allow increased bus capacities, as well as improved durability and longer service-lives. Improvements can be divided into four basic types: better maintenance for existing buses, better diesel buses and improved fuel quality, alternative-fuel buses, and advanced propulsion systems.

This chapter discusses alternative propulsion systems and fuels for urban transit buses, including options for the future. It compares their relative strengths and weaknesses in different applications and environments and addresses issues that transit agencies may face when considering appropriate engine technology. Each fuel and technology's current status, recent developments, extent of use, costs, emissions and efficiency characteristics are discussed. Diesel, CNG, LPG, DME, hybrid-electric and fuel-cell systems are reviewed.

DIESEL TECHNOLOGIES

Diesel engines are recognised and favoured worldwide for their fuel efficiency, excellent durability and low maintenance requirements. They offer the convenience of using a liquid fuel that is easily dispensed through an established fuelling infrastructure. The technology is mature, widely produced and competitively priced. Although diesel engines have historically produced high levels of pollutant emissions, especially oxides of nitrogen (NO_x) and particulate matter (PM), recent improvements in engines, fuel and emissions-control technology have resulted in new diesel systems for buses that are substantially cleaner than they were only a few years ago.

Emissions Control

Diesel exhaust remains a major concern in most countries, particularly emissions of fine particulates, oxides of nitrogen (NO_x) and toxic hydrocarbons. In developing countries, particulate matter (PM) of all sizes is often a major concern, and diesel vehicles are often a major source. There is considerable evidence that some components of diesel emissions are carcinogenic. The California Air Resources Board lists diesel PM as a toxic air contaminant, and the South Coast Air Quality Management District's MATES II study indicates a large amount of the air-borne cancer risk in the South Coast comes from diesel emissions (Mates, 1999).

Other problems with diesel exhaust are the volatile organic compounds (VOCs) that are present as solid and gaseous matter, and oxides of nitrogen (NO_x). The organic compounds are the result of incomplete combustion. Engines designed to run at higher temperatures consume this material more completely, but higher temperatures also increase NO_x emissions. Diesels running on high-sulphur fuel can also produce substantial amounts of sulphur oxides (SO_x) and sulphate particulates.

Older and poorly maintained diesel engines may produce large amounts of coarse particulate emissions, including black carbon smoke, which may be coated with dangerous, unburned volatile compounds. Modern diesel-engine technologies have been successful in limiting these larger PM emissions. Over 90% of particle emissions from newer engines are very fine, less than 2.5 microns in diameter. However, these fine particles are also dangerous and may be carcinogenic. On the positive side, gaseous hydrocarbon emissions from a diesel engine can be low, and carbon dioxide emissions from diesel engines are lower than from many other types of engine.

Because of growing concern around the world over vehicle emissions, diesel fuel is at the same turning point that gasoline was in the late 1980s, when regulators sought drastic reductions in emissions from gasoline-powered vehicles. Eventually, these reductions were achieved through a combination of reformulated gasoline, improved engine design and, most importantly, advanced exhaust after-treatment systems featuring improved catalytic converters. Through this combined approach, order-of-magnitude emissions reductions were obtained between the mid-1980s and 2000. This has allowed gasoline-powered vehicles to meet the same tight emissions standards in the US and Europe as "inherently clean" alternative-fuel vehicles, such as those running on compressed natural gas (CNG).

Tighter emission requirements for heavy-duty engines in OECD countries over the next five-to-ten years are expected to drive similar order-of-magnitude emission reductions in diesel engines. (NO_x and PM standards for buses in the US and the EU are shown in Table 3.1.) As with gasoline vehicles, the basic strategy being followed by governments and manufacturers is to combine fuel reformulation, in the form of much lower sulphur diesel fuel, engine improvements and advanced after-treatment systems. In particular, advanced catalytic converters incorporating particulate filters, combined with ultra-low-sulphur diesel fuel, offer the promise of very low particulate emissions. Exhaust gas recirculation systems and other new approaches may lower NO_x levels to those of other fuels. Diesel vehicles with these characteristics are commonly referred to as "clean diesel".

The Euro system of heavy-duty vehicle emissions standards (shown in Table 3.1 through 2010) is frequently referenced around the world and will be used throughout this book. The various Euro standards for buses, their dates of application in Europe and the approximate diesel vehicle and fuel requirements to meet these standards are shown in Table 3.2. Meeting these standards also involves using the appropriate diesel fuel, and the Euro system has required fuel providers to make available lower-sulphur diesel fuels in time to assist buses in meeting these standards.

Table 3.1 Bus Emissions Standards for NO_x and PM through 2010, US and EU (g/kWh)

Model Year	NO_x		PM	
	US	EU	US	EU
2000	5.8	5.0	0.075	0.1
2001	5.8	5.0	0.075	0.1
2002	5.8	5.0	0.075	0.1
2003	2.9	5.0	0.075	0.1
2004	2.9	5.0	0.075	0.1
2005	2.9	3.5	0.075	0.02
2006	2.9	3.5	0.075	0.02
2007	0.16	3.5	0.0075	0.02
2008	0.16	2.0	0.0075	0.02
2009	0.16	2.0	0.0075	0.02
2010	0.16	2.0	0.0075	0.02

Source: ECMT, 2001.

Note: Euro III standards are applicable from October, 2001, Euro IV from 2005 and Euro V from 2008. Euro V standards subject to revision during 2002.

Table 3.2 The "Euro" Standard System for Heavy-duty Vehicles

	Date	NO_x	PM	Emission control requirements
Euro II	1998	7.0	0.15	Minor diesel engine improvements, good maintenance, proper operating settings, and diesel fuel preferably with 500 ppm sulphur or less
Euro III	2000	5.0	0.10	Further engine improvements (e.g. closed loop system) and probably a diesel oxidation catalyst. NOx standard may require an EGR system
Euro IV	2005	3.5	0.02	Ultra-low sulphur diesel (<50 ppm) and a catalytic particulate filter, with additional NOx control such as advanced EGR
Euro V	2008	2.0	0.02	Further NO_x reduction such as NO_x adsorber or SCR technologies

Note: This table is based on the test cycles that accompany the Euro classification system and the availability of appropriate fuel. Individual countries should develop systems of standards that reflect local fuel quality and driving conditions.

Strategies to Reduce Particulate Emissions

In countries where most buses are older or poorly maintained, particulate and other emissions can be reduced substantially just by improving maintenance and tuning. Proper engine maintenance, repair and tuning are probably the most important and cost-effective steps developing countries can take to reduce diesel emissions, especially particulates. However, such steps may require strong government regulation and strict enforcement. For example, in some instances buses may be tuned to maximize engine power, which may result in higher fuel consumption or emissions than necessary. Regular inspection can help minimise this practice.

Diesel exhaust emissions can also be reduced to some degree just by using cleaner fuel, in particular by lowering the sulphur and aromatic content in diesel fuel. Sulphate particulates and SO_x are emitted in nearly direct proportion to the amount of sulphur in diesel fuel. The formation of other hydrocarbons and particulates is also reduced as the sulphur content is reduced. Lower aromatic levels can reduce NO_x emissions significantly.

Another important benefit of reducing fuel sulphur levels is that it enables the use of new, advanced after-treatment systems, which can reduce emissions even further, especially particulates. For example, a 1999 report by the Manufacturer of Emission Controls Association (MECA) compared emissions from a 1998 diesel bus engine using fuels with different sulphur levels and various after-treatment systems. One of the fuels contained 368 ppm sulphur, and another contained 54 ppm sulphur. The lower-sulphur fuel reduced PM emissions by approximately 14% with no after-treatment. When a catalyst-based diesel particulate filter (DPF) was used in combination with the lower-sulphur fuel, 72% reductions in PM were achieved.

An oxidation catalyst can generally be used with diesel fuel containing up to 1000 ppm (0.1%) sulphur, but the introduction of ultra-low-sulphur diesel (ULSD) fuel, usually defined as having lower than 50 ppm sulphur, enables the use of more highly active after-treatment catalysts. These catalysts operate effectively at lower temperatures and have a broader range of vehicle applications. As oxidation catalyst efficiency improves, emissions of carbon monoxide (CO) and many types of hydrocarbons, including VOCs, drop significantly.

The use of ULSD makes its greatest contribution by enabling the use of advanced particulate filters. Relatively new types of regenerating filters, such as the popular Johnson Matthey "continuously regenerating trap" (CRT™) system, trap particulate matter by filtering it out of the exhaust stream and then clean (or "regenerate") the filter using oxidation catalyst coatings to help burn off the particulate matter (Matthey, 2001). This avoids the problem of clogging, which plagued the first generation of particulate filters; it also limits the need for periodic cleaning. The catalyst oxidises NO to NO_2, in the process creating heat that destroys the soot trapped in the walls of the filter. The filters reduce diesel particulate emissions anywhere from 80% to 99%, i.e. one to two orders of magnitude. Since they include an oxidation catalyst, they also substantially reduce carbon monoxide and hydrocarbon emissions (MECA, 2000, 2000b).

A potential limitation of particulate filters, however, is that they can quickly deteriorate if the diesel fuel sulphur level is too high. Fuel with sulphur levels in the maximum range of 30 ppm-50 ppm are acceptable in most operating environments, but for maximum efficiency and reliability, with the greatest reduction in PM emissions, sulphur levels below 15 ppm are recommended (Johnson Matthey, 2001). The European Commission has proposed tightening the current planned regulations for ULSD to require wide availability of 10 ppm sulphur diesel beginning in 2005. As the sulphur level rises above that point, the exhaust temperature needed to ensure proper regeneration of the filter rises, and problems can occur, particularly for vehicles operating at low speeds and/or on flat terrain. For these reasons, "clean diesel" is only an effective solution for cities where ULSD fuel is available, and for buses that produce sufficiently high exhaust temperatures.

Diesel particulate filters can be designed for use on nearly any diesel engine, and several engine manufacturers now offer DPFs as an original equipment option. However, the performance of diesel particulate filters may vary depending on the age of the engine. Even with very-low-sulphur fuel, it is unclear under what conditions particulate filters can be retrofitted and successfully operated with older engines, since older engines may not present ideal operating conditions. For example, engines that burn lubricating oil at rates higher than normal specification are poor candidates for a DPF. On the other hand, in some European countries DPFs have been operating with ULSD on vehicles more than six years old with no problem (US EPA, 2000). Further tests need to be performed on a variety of older bus types and in a variety of operating conditions to determine the extent to which retrofits are feasible and to determine the fuel and maintenance requirements for the retrofit to be successful.

Even though the technology is still evolving and the availability of ULSD is limited, the attractive emission reductions made possible by diesel particulate filters are spurring a rapid increase in their use throughout the developed world – especially in Europe, which has the largest market for ULSD fuel. The two biggest manufacturers of diesel particulate filters, Johnson Matthey Corp. and Engelhard Corp., have installed over 15,000 particulate filter systems in Europe. Among notable users is the Paris bus authority, RATP, which operates 700 buses utilising such systems in combination with ultra-low-sulphur diesel fuel. These buses meet the Euro-III standard.

In North America, New York City Transit (NYCT) recently completed testing and has switched to ULSD for its entire diesel bus fleet. By the end of 2003 NYCT plans to retrofit catalytic filter systems on all diesel buses[11].

---

11   Dana Lowell, NYCT, personal communication.

Results from programmes like these indicate that the technologies appear to meet durability requirements and provide substantial reductions in CO, HC and PM. PM levels of all sizes are comparable to the low levels associated with CNG buses.

One major shortcoming of DPF systems is that they have relatively little effect on NO_x. Typically NO_x reductions are in the 0%-to-10% range, which is much less than the reduction levels that will be required to meet future NO_x standards in Europe or North America.

Figure 3.1 shows the results from tests conducted by NYCT, comparing three configurations of the same bus: 1) with an OEM oxidation catalyst, running on standard 350 ppm diesel fuel (as the basis for comparison), 2) with the oxidation catalyst and ULSD fuel, and 3) with ULSD fuel and a catalytic particulate filter (the Johnson Matthey CRT system) in place of the OEM catalyst. The results indicate that with ULSD and the filter system, reductions of 80-99% are achieved in CO, HC and PM, but virtually no NO_x reduction is achieved.

Figure 3.1 Results of NYCT Diesel Bus Emissions Tests
(Percentage change relative to a "base" option of OEM catalyst and 350 ppm Sulphur fuel)

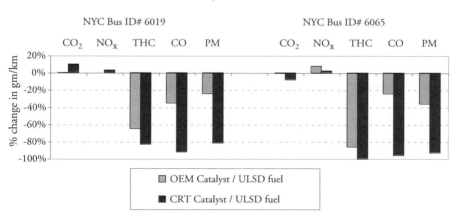

Source: Lanni *et al*, 2001. Note: THC = total hydrocarbons.

The European Commission's Jupiter-2 project recently examined the effects of continuously regenerating diesel particulate filters used with ULSD on vehicular emissions in Merseyside, UK. The project found impacts similar to NYCT, as shown in Table 3.3. The project also found DPFs to be a particularly cost-effective way to reduce emissions, since the systems cost about $5,000 per bus with little other infrastructure requirements. Associated fuel costs (discussed below) also appear likely to be reasonable.

Table 3.3 Findings from the Jupiter 2 Project

Exhaust components	Exhaust emissions in "13 Mode Circle" (g/kWh)		Exhaust emissions in "Munich Circle" (g/kWh)	
	without CRT	with CRT	Without CRT	with CRT
CO	0.58	0.04	0.9	0.02
HC	0.26	0.002	0.63	0.01
NO$_x$	5.62	5.21	6.48	6.41
PM	0.127	0.01	0.127	0.013

Source: Jupiter 2000.

Strategies to Reduce NO$_x$

Since conventional oxidation catalysts and catalyst-filter systems will not provide sufficient reductions to reach the lower NO$_x$ standards for heavy duty-vehicles that will be phased in for developed countries over the next 10 years (Table 3.2) – especially the very tight NO$_x$ standard for the US – a separate strategy for NO$_x$ emissions is needed.

Several approaches to NO$_x$ control are under development, including advanced exhaust gas recovery (EGR) systems, lean-NO$_x$ catalysts, NO$_x$ adsorber catalysts, and urea-based selective catalytic reduction (SCR) devices. A summary of each method is provided below. Estimated impacts on NO$_x$ and on fuel economy are presented in Table 3.4.

Table 3.4 NO$_x$-reduction Measures

	NO$_x$ reduction (%)	Fuel economy impact
EGR system	40-60%	Possibly slight improvement
Lean NO$_x$ catalyst	20-30%	5% or greater reduction
NO$_x$ adsorption	90% or better	2-5% reduction
SCR system	65-99%	Uncertain

Lean-NO$_x$ catalysts have been under development for a number of years, but improvements appear to be diminishing. They appear unlikely to provide more than about a 30% reduction in NO$_x$, not nearly enough to meet the future US or European standards, at least not without help from other methods. The catalysts also may reduce fuel efficiency by five percent or more (Lloyd and Cackette, 2001).

Exhaust gas recovery (EGR) systems reroute a portion of the exhaust gas stream to the engine air intake. This dilutes the air with inert exhaust gas, reducing flame temperatures when fuel is ignited and lowering formation of NO$_x$. Well-designed EGR systems can reduce NO$_x$ from the tailpipe by 30% to 50%. Advanced systems can do even better through more careful control and variation of the gas recovery rate under different driving conditions (Detroit Diesel, 2000).

NO$_x$ Adsorber systems have shown potential for large reductions in NO$_x$ emissions (US DOE, 2000, 2000b), but are very sensitive to the sulphur level in fuel and may require near-zero-sulphur fuels to function properly (MECA, 2000). The NO$_x$ adsorber catalyst works by temporarily storing NO$_x$ on the absorbent during normal engine operation. When the absorbent becomes saturated, engine operation and fuel delivery rates are temporarily adjusted to produce a fuel-rich exhaust, which converts and releases the NO$_x$ as N$_2$. These techniques can reduce NO$_x$ emissions by more than 90%, but the process reduces fuel economy slightly (Lloyd and Cackette, 2001). To date, no NO$_x$ adsorber system has proven commercially feasible.

Selective Catalytic Reduction (SCR) is another process under development, which involves injecting a liquid urea solution into the exhaust before it reaches a catalyst. The urea then breaks down and reacts with NO$_x$ to produce nitrogen and water. Using the SCR system, it might be possible to meet future NO$_x$ emission standards without ultra-low-sulphur diesel fuel (although without ULSD fuel the PM emission standard may not be attainable). SCR systems are estimated to provide NO$_x$ reductions from 65% to 99% depending on operating conditions. While the SCR approach is promising, a number of issues remain to be addressed. For example, there is currently no infrastructure for distributing urea to refuelling centres or system for ensuring the proper restocking of urea on board vehicles.

The US EPA considers NO_x adsorbers to be the NO_x emission-control technology most likely to succeed, despite the sulphur sensitivity and the potential reduction in fuel efficiency (US EPA, 2000b). The EPA believes that additional improvements will allow vehicles with adsorber systems to meet the 2007 US emission standards for heavy-duty diesel engines and eliminate the current fuel economy penalty.

Availability and Cost of Ultra-Low-Sulphur Diesel Fuel

Although ultra-low-sulphur (<50 ppm) diesel fuel is a key to reducing diesel PM emissions, its availability is currently limited to small markets, primarily in Europe and to a lesser extent in the United States. This is set to change in Europe, where its use is expanding rapidly. By 2003 a number of countries (including Sweden, the UK, Germany and the Netherlands) will have converted to ULSD for all on-road diesel fuel. Despite these early indications that fuel producers are willing to expand deliveries of ULSD, the rest of the world will have to wait and will have to continue wringing out emission reductions with high-sulphur fuels. In most of the developed world, standard on-road diesel fuel contains 350-500 ppm sulphur (off-road diesel has up to 10 times as much). In the developing world, the situation is even worse; diesel fuel commonly contains more than one thousand ppm sulphur (1000 ppm sulphur is equal to 0.1% sulphur by weight). However, many countries have recently taken initiatives to reduce diesel-fuel sulphur content and in a growing number of countries the level has been or will soon be lowered below 1000 ppm (Lubrizol, 2002).

The technology for reducing sulphur in diesel fuel to maximum 15 ppm is currently available, and new technologies are under development that could reduce the cost of desulphurisation in the refinery process. However, making ULSD will require huge refinery investments that some companies may not be able or willing to make for a secondary product. In reasonably high-volume production, ULSD is projected to cost anywhere from one to four US cents more per litre (US EIA, 2001) than conventional diesel – with costs at the higher end of this range in cases where the fuel must be brought in from a distant refinery. Cost may also be higher during transition phases, if the demand for ULSD temporarily outstrips supply.

With the European Union enacting regulations that will limit the level of fuel sulphur to 50 ppm, and possibly 10 ppm, beginning in 2005, most of Europe is expected to convert to ULSD over the coming years. In the United States, the Environmental Protection Agency has proposed a rule requiring refiners and importers to produce 80% of highway diesel containing a maximum of 15 ppm starting 1 June, 2006. Under the proposal, up to 20% of highway diesel fuel may continue to meet the current 500 ppm sulphur limit until May 2010.

In the developing world, where ULSD is not currently available from national refiners and may not be for some time, shifting to ULSD will be even more challenging. In India, for example, recent legislation has only sought to reduce the sulphur content of diesel fuel to a maximum of 500 ppm. Although this is a major reduction from previous levels above 1000 ppm, it is far from the 50 ppm level necessary to support advanced emission-reduction technologies. The Tata Energy Research Institute (TERI) recently completed a study which estimates that in India ULSD for buses would be considerably less expensive than CNG on a per-kilometre basis, taking into account refining upgrade costs, fuel distribution and refuelling infrastructure, and retailing (but not bus costs). They estimated an average cost of Rs2.9 ($0.06) per kilometre for ULSD v. CNG at Rs4.4 (0.09$US) per kilometre (TERI, 2001). ULSD would currently need to be imported, but is available from large regional refining centres such as Singapore.

Prospects for Retrofitting Emissions Control on Existing Buses

An important consideration for bus operators around the world is whether advanced emissions-control equipment can be successfully retrofitted onto existing buses without adversely affecting engine performance. The ability to apply these technologies to existing diesels is critical for two reasons. First, older engines pollute much more than newer ones and remain on the road for decades (MECA, 2001); cleaning them up is imperative. Second, it costs less for transit agencies to invest in retrofits than to purchase new buses.

The scope for achieving emissions reductions through retrofits is enormous. In the United States, for example, the EPA estimates that retrofitting 10,000 heavy-duty engines is not only possible, but could eliminate roughly 15,000 tons of harmful pollution each year. Transit agencies must proceed strategically, however. Since most retrofit emission control technologies are adversely affected by sulphur in the fuel, localities must ensure that suitable fuel is available. It will be important to work with technology suppliers to determine exactly what type of fuel is required. In some cases, transit agencies might need to form partnerships with energy companies to ensure delivery of high-quality fuel.

Hong Kong's Retrofit Program

In Hong Kong, where there are 12,000 diesel buses, half of which are pre-Euro-standard, the government has undertaken a programme beginning in 2000 to test particulate filters and diesel oxidation catalysts. In its 1999 Policy Statement, the government decided that the installation of catalytic converters and filters was the most practical way to reduce emissions from these old diesel vehicles (Hong Kong, 1999).

The franchised bus companies have started to install such devices in their older vehicles, and the government has been conducting trials to identify oxidation catalysts that are suitable for other types of medium and heavy diesel vehicles. About 1,000 vehicles have been retrofitted with particulate filters and 100 vehicles with oxidation catalysts. The government is providing financial assistance of about $1,300 per vehicle to offset installation costs for this equipment. Equipment costs for the more expensive oxidation catalysts and filters are estimated between $4,000 and $7,500, depending on engine size and the catalyst model. Eventually the installation of particulate filters or catalytic converters will be required to renew registration of all pre-Euro-standard diesel vehicles (Hong Kong, 2000).

In addition, like many European countries, Hong Kong adopted the more stringent Euro III emission standard from 2001, after which no new diesel vehicle may be imported unless it complies with this standard. Hong Kong has also introduced ULSD fuel and has provided strong incentives for its use. In 2000, the Government adopted an incentive program involving a concessionary duty on ULSD of HK$1.11 per litre (89 cents less than regular diesel). This was to be charged until January 1, 2001, and then increased to $2.00, the same duty as for regular diesel (Dieselnet, 2000).

Retrofitting of diesel oxidation catalysts (DOCs) on off-road vehicles has been taking place for over 20 years, particularly in the underground mining industry, where over 250,000 engines have been retrofitted. Since 1995, over 20,000 DOC systems have been retrofitted on buses and trucks in the United States and Europe. Over 3,000 trucks and buses have been retrofitted in Mexico. Hong Kong has begun to retrofit thousands of urban buses with DOCs (MECA 2001). Since many oxidation catalysts can be used with diesel fuel with up to 1,000 ppm sulphur, this can be one of the most widely applicable retrofit options for the developing world.

Even retrofitting vehicles with the more advanced catalytic particulate filter systems is not especially difficult if the vehicle is suitable and ULSD fuel is available. Including the cost of materials, retrofits typically cost $4,000 to $8,000 per vehicle and can take as little as two hours to conduct. As long as the engine exhaust temperatures are adequate and the correct fuel is used (ULSD), the filter systems can be employed. They generally do not significantly alter engine performance or reliability. Catalyst-filter manufacturers can design and fabricate them based on the exhaust-system specifications of the target vehicles. Manufacturers also may work with fleet operators to evaluate the condition of the engines and monitor engine exhaust temperatures during normal operation. This process can take up to 60 days, although such testing does not interrupt normal use of the vehicles. Final installation of the catalytic particulate filter can often be performed by the fleet's maintenance personnel during regularly scheduled maintenance (ARCO, 2001).

In Sweden, over 6,500 diesel buses have been retrofitted with catalytic particulate filter systems. DPFs have also been retrofitted on heavy-duty vehicles in Great Britain, Germany, Finland, Denmark and France. In off-road applications, over 10,000 filter systems have been retrofitted on diesel engines over the past ten years. In the United States, diesel filter retrofit programmes are under way in California and in New York City, which plans to retrofit 3,500 buses with DPF's (MECA, 2001).

Selective catalytic reduction systems (SCR), using urea as a reducing agent, have also been retrofitted onto diesel-powered vehicles, with impressive results. They provide reductions in NO_x of 75% to 90%, in HC of 50% to 90%, and in PM of 30% to 50%. Diesel engines used on marine vessels, ferries and locomotives have also been retrofitted. Some have operated satisfactorily for over eight years. Currently, over 40 diesel engines have been retrofitted with SCR in Europe. A programme in Germany where 22 line-haul trucks were fitted with SCR systems, achieved its reduction targets of approximately 70% NO_x, 80% HC and 30% PM. The fleet accumulated a combined 5.8 million kilometres of operation. Several vehicles ran over 400,000 kilometres with excellent results (MECA, 2001).

New systems which combine catalysts, filters, air enhancement technologies, thermal management technologies and/or engine adjustments and components are emerging as retrofit options. A combined emission-control system using ceramic engine coatings combined with fuel injection timing retard and an oxidation catalyst has produced more than a 40% reduction in NO_x while maintaining very low particulate emissions. The system has been approved under the US EPA urban bus rebuild/retrofit programme (MECA 2001).

Considerations in Adopting Clean-Diesel Programmes

From the findings above, it is evident that the new advanced "clean-diesel" engines, using ULSD and incorporating a catalytic particulate filter, can dramatically reduce the levels of diesel emissions. Moreover, as discussed below, alternatives such as CNG often cost more. As a result, many transit agencies have concluded that "clean diesel" yields sufficient emissions reductions while preserving the advantages and cost-savings of diesel fuel systems.

For agencies and companies considering the clean diesel option, a number of additional factors should be considered:

■ The lifetime pollutant emissions of buses using ULSD and advanced after-treatment systems are still highly uncertain, especially in cities with uncertain fuel supplies or harsh operating environments. The risk of fuel adulteration should be considered, since diesel particulate filter systems can be severely damaged by even a small amount of high-sulphur diesel fuel (or kerosene).

■ Although clean diesel provides impressive emissions reductions, its contribution to sustainable transport is limited by the fact that it does little to reduce oil use.

- Continued reliance on diesel fuel does little to prepare for the potential future switch to advanced fuels – particularly to gaseous fuels, such as hydrogen. Working with advanced diesel engines with electronic control systems may, however, provide transit agencies and bus companies with experience to help prepare them for a later switch to electric-drive-train systems, such as those used in hybrid-electric and fuel-cell buses.

The desire to minimise expenditures on maintenance and fuel is a strong driver in virtually all transportation businesses, and urban transit agencies are no exception. In the developing world, "balancing the books" is even more of a challenge for transit agencies. Low fares and revenues make it difficult to buy new buses or even to improve old ones. In Delhi, for example, diesel buses are currently manufactured to Euro-I norms, for roughly Rs 1,700,000 ($34,000). Manufacturing "advanced" diesel buses which comply with Euro-II norms would require significant engine modifications to increase the pressure of the fuel-injection system and introduce variable injection timing and turbo charging. This may cost between Rs 50,000 and Rs 100,000 ($1,000 to $2,000), depending on whether turbo chargers are already standard equipment (Delhi, 2001). To reduce particulates and other emissions consistent with Euro-IV standards, will require electronic fuel-injection systems, exhaust gas re-circulation, catalytic converters and particulate filters in addition to turbo charging. These additional features will require large additional investments.

Furthermore, the developing world is often the recipient of second-hand technologies which have been modified to maximise fuel efficiency — at the expense of environmental performance. In other words, starting from pre-Euro or even Euro-1 levels, it will take a big effort to adopt clean diesel successfully. In some cases, a commitment to a completely new fuel/vehicle system may be simpler, although such commitments entail complexities of their own.

WATER-IN-OIL EMULSIONS

Water-in-oil emulsions used as motor fuels have existed for at least 100 years. However, companies have only recently been able to control the stability and quality of the emulsion to make it practical for use in a diesel engine. While there is still uncertainty about the emission-reduction potential of these fuels, significant reductions in NO_x and PM have been demonstrated in comparison testing with conventional diesel fuels. Further reductions in total emissions have been achieved through the combination of water-fuel blend with an oxidation catalyst and particulate filter. These have even been demonstrated to outperform ultra-low-sulphur diesel in some tests (CARB, 2000).

The primary benefit of diesel/water emulsion fuels is that they are "fill-and-go" technologies that instantly reduce emissions from existing diesel-powered engines and vehicles, without the need for significant vehicle modifications. In the developing world, these emulsions have the advantage of improving emissions for vehicles of virtually any age or condition, with minimal investment or learning.

Technology Status

Several companies, such as TotalFinaElf, A-55 and Lubrizol Corp., market products that allow oil/water emulsions to be stable enough for use in diesel engines. These products allow engines to tolerate fuel blends with 5% to 30% water, although 10% water is the most common. The specifications of these products vary but their principal is similar: the blend additive surrounds diesel and/or water droplets to allow a stable mixture and prevent the water from separating out of the fuel. The encapsulation produces a fuel blend that is stable for several months and ensures that no water will contact metal engine parts, therefore avoiding engine corrosion.

In some cases sale of the product includes provision of an entire system of mixing and storing the diesel/water emulsion that can be installed at local oil storage or distribution centres (such as bus company diesel fuel holding tank areas). Mixing systems, such as one offered by Lubrizol, perform several tasks: they purify the water to a specification necessary for optimal performance in a blend, mix it with diesel oil in an electronically controlled, automated blending unit to produce a stable, finished fuel, and ensure that no separation of the blend occurs during storage.

The presence of water in the emulsion reduces both PM and NO_x emissions in diesel engines. The water lowers combustion temperature, which reduces NO_x emissions. To a point, the greater the water content of the emulsion, the greater the NO_x reductions. The water also produces a different combustion pattern, which causes the carbon in the fuel to burn more completely, producing lower diesel PM emissions.

Diesel/water emulsions appear to provide substantial reductions in certain emissions in comparison with conventional diesel fuel, without after-treatment. Estimates of anywhere from 20% to 80% reductions in PM and "smoke" and 10% to 30% reductions in NO_x have been reported. In January 2001, the California Air Resources Board (CARB) officially ascribed to Lubrizol's PuriNOx blend fuel a 14 % reduction in nitrogen oxides and a 63% reduction in particulate matter (Lubrizol, 2001).

A set of recently published tests using the Lubrizol emulsion with a 10% water blend indicated that it compares favourably with ULSD and equivalent emission-control systems (Barnes *et al*, 2000). As shown in the test results in Table 3.5, water-blend fuel provided results similar to ULSD (50ppm) under several configurations – without any emissions-control equipment, with an oxidising catalytic converter and with a particulate filter (but no converter). Both provide significant reductions in HC and CO when combined with a catalyst, and in PM when combined with a particulate filter. The water-blend formula in these tests reduced NO_x by about 10% relative to ULSD, regardless of after-treatment. This is only one set of tests with one particular formula, but the results indicate that water-blend fuels can compete with ULSD in emissions benefits.

The IEA has seen no test results indicating whether there are any problems with the use of diesel/water blends with catalysts and, especially, particulate filters over a range of operating conditions and over the life of a vehicle.

Table 3.5 Emissions from Test Buses Operating on Ultra-low Sulphur Diesel (ULSD) and Water-blend Fuel (WBF)
(grams per kilometre)

	HC	CO	NO_x /10	CO2/1000	PM
ULSD	0.882	2.04	1.85	1.82	0.238
WBF	0.866	2.09	1.68	1.78	0.166
ULSD+cat	0.046	0.07	1.81	1.83	0.192
WBF+cat	0.063	0.07	1.54	1.69	0.115
ULSD+trap	0.829	2.14	1.86	1.87	0.045
WBF+trap	0.777	2.01	1.62	1.72	0.028

Source: Barnes et al, 2000.

Note: "cat" is oxidation catalyst; "trap" is particulate filter.

Further tests may be useful to determine whether any such compatibility problems exist.

In addition to its effects on emissions, mixing water with diesel fuel has several other impacts on the performance of the fuel, but none appears to be major. There is commonly a slight loss in engine power at full throttle, although testing has shown that power and torque curves with the emulsions are comparable to those with standard diesel fuel. The impact of the power loss appears to depend particularly upon the engine/vehicle duty cycle and could range from zero to 15% for 20% water-based fuels. Losses would be lower in slower urban driving cycles – typical for many buses.

The presence of water decreases the volumetric energy content, which is translated into a reduction in fuel economy as measured by distance per volumetric unit of fuel use. However, the emulsion results in little difference, or perhaps a slight improvement, in fuel efficiency, as measured by distance per unit energy use.

The cost of diesel/water blends appears slightly higher than a comparable volume of diesel fuel. In comparing one litre of emulsion fuel versus one litre of diesel, the cost of emulsion must include the emulsifying additive, blending hardware and an anti-freeze component for water during winter in cold climates. But the blend replaces part of the diesel with water at virtually no cost. On balance, the cost increase slightly outweighs the decrease. Including taxes, if the water portion of the new diesel/water/emulsion is taxed at the same rate as pure diesel, a 10% water emulsion would be 5% to 15% more expensive than diesel. If the water portion is not taxed, the emulsion would cost anywhere from three percent less to five percent more than regular diesel. If emulsion fuel is taxed at a lower rate (to reflect its lower environmental impact, as is currently done in France and Italy), emulsion can cost less than diesel (Lubrizol, 2001).

Demonstration Projects

As part of its "Bus Ecologique" programme, Paris RATP currently uses the diesel/water blend "Aquasol" (developed by TotalFinaElf) in 300 of its older buses. Aquasol is an emulsion of diesel fuel (85%) and water (13%), with two percent additives. RATP has found that Aquasol reduces NO_x emissions by 30% and virtually eliminates visible smoke emissions. RATP, however, does not plan to use Aquasol on newer buses. After the older buses are retired, it intends to replace them with diesel buses using ULSD and catalysed particulate filters (RATP, 2001), in order to reach even lower emissions levels and meet Euro-III standards.

Italy's third-largest fuel and lubricant marketer, Kuwait Petroleum Italia (KPIT), recently signed a contract with the Lubrizol Corporation to market PuriNOx fuel under the name "Q White". During 2001, KPIT leased and installed three Lubrizol blending units required to prepare the PuriNOx fuel-water emulsion. KPIT will invest $1 million and will distribute Q White to owners of vehicle fleets and other diesel-powered equipment in Italy. Of the estimated 16,900-kiloton diesel market in Italy, KPIT projects an 850-kiloton market for emulsion fuels such as Q White, primarily public service buses. According to KPIT, there is an approximately $1.75 billion, non-retail diesel-fuel market in Italy. The company plans to target almost 10% of this market with the Q White technology. This commercialisation effort was reinforced by a European Commission decision authorising Italy to apply reduced excise duty to water/diesel emulsions from 1 October, 2000 until 31 December, 2005. The Italian Ministry of Finance has also designated a 36% lower tax rate for emulsion fuels than for conventional diesel fuel. This tax category applies to stabilised emulsion fuels meeting the specification set by the Italian government in March 2000.

India has been testing the endurance of diesel engines operating on water-diesel emulsions. The tests were carried out on a four-stroke diesel engine with pure diesel and 10 per cent water-diesel emulsions and it was determined that no abnormal wear occurred with the use of emulsified fuel (Reddy and Prasad, 2000). Emulsions in Indian buses provided up to 40% NO_x and 60% particulate matter reductions compared to buses on conventional diesel fuel.

Considerations in Using Diesel/Water Emulsions

Several factors must be considered in deciding whether to use diesel/water blend fuels for buses:

- Pre-emulsified fuels require sizeable investments for preparation, distribution and storage prior to refuelling. However, the emulsion product companies appear prepared to assist in financing and setting up the necessary infrastructure.

- Use of water-emulsified diesel fuel could result in a drop in engine power, depending upon such factors as the water content of the fuel, operating conditions and engine settings.

- Vehicles must carry the water component of the fuel, resulting in reduced range, extra weight or extra refuelling. This may imply extra costs.

- If vehicles are not operated for several months, some separation of the water and diesel components in fuel emulsions could occur, resulting in start-up problems.

BIODIESEL AND BLENDS

Biodiesel is an ester-based oxygenated diesel fuel made from vegetable oil or animal fats. It can be produced from oilseed plants such as soybeans and rapeseed, or from used vegetable oil. It has similar properties to petroleum-based diesel fuel and can be blended into petroleum-based diesel fuel at any ratio for use with conventional diesel engines. It is most often blended into petroleum-based diesel fuel at 20%. This mixture is commonly referred to as "B20". Pure biodiesel is termed B100 or "neat".

Although biodiesel is similar to petroleum-based diesel, there are some significant differences. Biodiesel contains 11% oxygen by weight and contains no sulphur or aromatic hydrocarbons. On a transient test cycle, fuel economy and power with neat biodiesel are about 10% lower than with conventional diesel fuel; with B20 the loss is about two percent. Biodiesel has favourable lubricity characteristics, but will soften and degrade certain types of rubber compounds over time. Manufacturers recommend that natural or butyl rubbers not come in contact with pure biodiesel. Biodiesel can be stored in the same tanks as petroleum-based diesel, but it has a shorter shelf life, which makes it less suitable for use in emergency generators or engines that operate infrequently (CARB, 2000).

Emission data comparing biodiesel with conventional diesel are limited. Most tests focus on B20. Tests of B20 show about 30% reductions in particulates and about 50% reductions in hydrocarbon emissions (if an oxidation catalyst is used), but essentially no NO_x reduction (CARB, 2000). At higher blend levels, there is some evidence that NO_x emissions can increase significantly.

Unless biodiesel comprises at least 90% of the fuel blend, when mixed with standard diesel fuel (at 350-500 ppm sulphur), it will not reduce the diesel sulphur content sufficiently to allow application of advanced control strategies, such as particulate filters and NO_x adsorbers, that require ultra-low-sulphur diesel fuel.

Over the past ten years biodiesel fuels have commonly cost two to three times as much as conventional diesel, although using a 20% blend dampens this cost difference, placing it in the range of some other clean fuels. But biodiesel blends are quite expensive relative to ultra-low-sulphur diesel and may not enable as much reduction in NO_x and PM. On the other hand, biodiesel displaces petroleum while ULSD does not. Biodiesel can also provide GHG reductions of 30% or more compared to regular or ultra-low-sulphur diesel (IEA/AFIS, 1999).

Considerations in Using Biodiesel

Several factors should be considered when deciding whether to use biodiesel blend fuels for buses:

- Biodiesel fuels burn like diesel fuels and are compatible with conventional diesel engines, and do not adversely affect payload, freight volume or vehicle range.

- Waste oils, such as used cooking oils, might be used to make biodiesel cheaper than biodiesel produced directly from crops, although volumes are likely to be small.

- Since it is blendable with current diesel fuel, biodiesel may be easier to use than other alternative fuels such as compressed natural gas or LPG. However, it may be more expensive and provide fewer pollutant emissions reductions than other alternative fuels.

- It provides more greenhouse gas reductions than many other options.

COMPRESSED NATURAL GAS

The challenge of trying to squeeze more and more pollution reductions from trucks and buses, already subject to rigorous controls in the developed world, has led to a continuing search for viable alternative fuels and propulsion systems. Foremost among these is natural gas, which can be used today in conventional vehicles powered by slightly modified internal combustion engines. Like clean diesel, natural gas can provide immediate air quality benefits. However, over the longer term, natural gas may also be a bridge to advanced technologies utilising gaseous fuels – such as hydrogen fuel cells.

Unlike diesel fuel, which is a mixture of many different hydrocarbon compounds, natural gas is a simple hydrocarbon fossil fuel that typically contains 85% to 99% methane (CH_4) and near-zero sulphur. It is naturally clean-burning, and in many countries relatively abundant and inexpensive. Several bus manufacturers offer high-quality CNG buses, and many bus conversions from diesel to CNG have been performed in various cities, although with a mixed record of performance.

Natural gas has a number of shortcomings as a vehicle fuel. Due to the very low energy density of methane, the gas must be compressed for on-board storage in large, expensive cylinders, weighing as much as several thousand pounds. These factors plus required engine modifications can make CNG buses significantly more expensive than diesel buses, even "clean-diesel" buses. In addition, the CNG refuelling infrastructure for a bus system can cost millions of dollars, depending on the existing fuel-supply infrastructure and local regulations for safe storage and refuelling.

Natural gas can be combusted in an internal combustion engine in a number of ways including stoichiometric (spark-ignited, fuel and air mixed to achieve complete combustion), lean-burn (also spark-ignited, but using more air) and dual-fuel with diesel (compression-ignited, also primarily lean-burn). Most of the "original equipment" (OEM) CNG buses offered today in the United States have lean-burn engines to minimise NO_x emissions without NO_x after-treatment. CNG buses converted from diesel buses, however, often produce relatively high NO_x. All CNG-fuelled buses have low levels of PM emissions.

The potential benefits of natural gas have stimulated many tests comparing CNG buses with diesel buses in terms of emissions, fuel economy, reliability and cost – with a confusing array of findings. Some studies have found that CNG buses provide dramatic reductions in emissions relatively cheaply, while others have found quite the opposite. These variations are due, in part, to two important differences among studies:

■ **Date of study and vintage of buses.** Five year-old studies comparing new CNG buses with new diesel buses (and new studies comparing five-year old buses) tend to show a bigger environmental advantage for CNG buses than studies of recent model buses. Some studies also compare buses of differing vintages, such as newer CNG buses and older diesel buses.

■ **Emissions-control equipment.** A comparison of CNG and diesel buses with no emissions-control equipment will tend to show substantial emissions reductions with CNG, since it is inherently cleaner than diesel. Adding a basic oxidation catalyst to the diesel bus closes the gap somewhat, but not much (and such a catalyst can also be added to a CNG bus). When the diesel bus uses ULSD and a catalytic particulate filter, most studies estimate that emissions of several major pollutants (CO, hydrocarbons and PM) from the diesel bus are as low as a comparable CNG bus. A properly optimised CNG bus may still win out on NO_x, but it is likely that diesels equipped with advanced NO_x reduction systems will eventually compete with the best CNG buses.

As diesel technologies improve, any emissions advantage currently held by new CNG buses will likely diminish, making it even more difficult for transit agencies to choose the "optimal technology path" to meet increasingly strict emissions standards. Life-cycle emissions analysis may become increasingly important in making choices. CNG buses have the advantage of less reliance on emission-control systems that can wear out or be removed, and no reliance on low-sulphur fuels, which can be limited in supply or adulterated. However, although NO_x emissions from new CNG buses are naturally lower than from diesel buses, they can be very high if buses are not properly maintained.

INFORM (2000) reviewed the results of nine recent testing programmes that compared emissions from conventional diesel and CNG buses. Most of the studies compared vehicles made in the mid-to-late 1990s, and none of the tested diesel vehicles used ULSD or were equipped with a particulate filter. It is unclear how many of the diesel vehicles were equipped with standard oxidation catalysts. CNG buses were found to emit anywhere from 40% to 86% less particulate matter and 38% to 58% less nitrogen oxide than diesel buses. However, NO_x emissions varied widely, and in a few cases well-tuned diesel engines emitted less NO_x than poorly tuned CNG engines.

Results from a study conducted by West Virginia University (NAVC, 1999) are typical of the studies reviewed by the INFORM study. As shown in Table 3.6, CNG buses produced much lower NO_x and PM emissions than comparable diesel buses. The diesels had much lower CO and hydrocarbon emissions than the CNG buses. CO emissions are not a serious concern in most cities, and most of the CNG hydrocarbon emissions are non-reactive methane, which is not an important pollutant although it is a potent greenhouse gas.

Table 3.6 Comparison of Emissions from CNG and Standard Diesel Engines (grams per mile)

Bus (engine)	PM	NO_x	HC	CO	CO_2
Orion CNG (Detroit Diesel – Series 50G)	0.007	11.2	26.2	9.38	2,656
Orion CNG (Detroit Diesel – Series 50G)	0.022	9.19	31.6	13.5	2,832
Orion CNG (Detroit Diesel – Series 50G)	0.041	8.79	20.6	9.59	2,867
Nova Diesel (Detroit Diesel – Series 50G)	0.32	38.0	0.02	2.95	3,213
Nova Diesel (Detroit Diesel – Series 50G)	0.21	41.5	0.06	2.95	3,122
Nova Diesel (Detroit Diesel – Series 50G)	0.15	36.9	0.04	2.27	2,837

Source: NAVC, 1999.
Note: Three separate Orion CNG and three separate Nova diesel buses were tested, accounting for the different results.

Although CNG provides clear reductions in NO_x and PM compared with regular diesel buses, this advantage may disappear when compared with "clean-diesel" buses operating on ULSD with catalytic particulate filters. While few cities have conducted detailed comparisons, at least two have: New York and Paris. Both cities found that clean-diesel buses produce emissions comparable to CNG buses. Some of the New York test results are presented in Figure 3.2. In these comparisons, the diesel buses (labelled "CRT", after the type of particulate filter used) came close to the CNG-bus levels of PM and NO_x, especially taking into account the variation around the mean (denoted by the vertical lines banding the bars). Similar results have been found in Paris (RATP, 2001).

FIGURE 3.2 Comparison of CRT/ULSD Diesel and CNG Buses by NY City Transit Agency

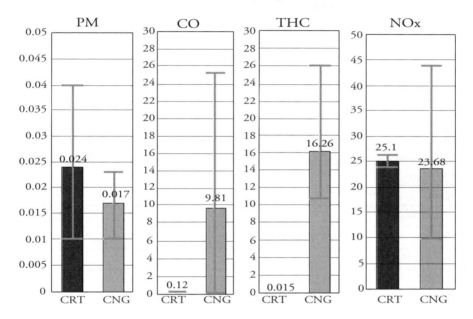

Source: NYS-DEC *et al*, 2001.

Notes: diesel buses were equipped with a catalytic filter and tested on ULSD; diesel and CNG buses were of comparable age and were tested on the same duty cycle.

Some studies also indicate that natural-gas vehicles may emit a greater number of ultra-fine particles than "clean" diesel vehicles, and that these smaller particles may be the most significant threat to human health (Holmén *et al*, 2001; Lloyd and Cackette, 2001). But this is still an area of intensive research.

One area where CNG buses may not outperform even regular diesel buses is greenhouse gas emissions. CO_2 emissions from CNG buses are typically equal to or lower than diesel. However, when upstream emissions of various greenhouse gases, particularly methane, are included, some studies estimate that CNG buses produce significantly more total GHG emissions than diesel buses (UK, 2000). Life-cycle emissions vary from country to country due to differences in vehicle efficiencies, upstream efficiencies, fuel supply sources, etc. In particular, upstream emissions of methane can vary considerably depending on the length and conditions of natural gas pipelines. A life-cycle study specific to each city or country is probably needed to reliably determine, in that context, the net impacts of one vehicle technology or fuel type compared to another.

CNG Buses in Operation

Throughout Europe and North America, transit agencies have significantly increased their number of CNG buses in recent years. Table 3.7 shows that

Table 3.7 CNG Buses in Europe

Total Number of CNG Buses

Country	1996	Present	Known Purchase Plans through 2006
Austria	0	4	3
Belgium	25	53	4
Czech Republic	5	86	70
Finland	0	29	NA
France	1	208	350
Germany	46	464	91
Greece	NA	295	NA
Italy	23	579	NA
Ireland	0	1	NA
The Netherlands	12	1	NA
Norway	0	13	60
Poland	6	17	NA
Portugal	NA	118	150
Russia	NA	278	NA
Spain	17	65	NA
Sweden	91	318	2
Switzerland	12	29	NA
Total	238	2558	730

Source: ENGVA, 2001. NA = not available. Data for U.K. are unavailable, but numbers are believed to be very low.

the number of CNG buses in service in European countries has grown ten-fold since 1996 (ENGVA, 2001).

In the United States, the recent trend toward CNG bus use has also been strong. A recent American Public Transit Association (APTA) survey indicates strong growth over the past several years, in part because a number of transit authorities have made a commitment to purchase a large number of natural-gas buses – in some cases to the exclusion of diesel buses. APTA's 1999 Transit Vehicle Data Book shows:

- Compared to 1998, the number of CNG buses on order grew by 26% from 890 to 1,125.

- Of the potential orders where fuel type has been specified, the share of natural gas buses grew from 16% in 1998 to 31% in 1999 (from 2,100 to 4,079).

- Since 1998, the total number of agencies that operate natural gas vehicles grew by 14% from 57 to 65, and the total number of natural gas buses in operation grew by 28% from 2,494 to 3,204.

- Eighteen transit agencies now operate a third or more of their fleet on natural gas. These agencies are located in Tempe, AZ; Thousand Palms, CA; San Diego, CA; Oxnard, CA; State College, PA; Boise, ID; Sacramento, CA; Fort Worth, TX; Laredo, TX; El Paso, TX; Garden City, NY; Tucson, AZ; Culver City, CA; Port Huron, MI; Tacoma, WA; Phoenix, AZ (two agencies – the Regional Public Transit Authority and the City of Phoenix Public Transit Department); and Davis, CA.

- Ten transit agencies now have over 100 natural gas buses operating in their fleet. These agencies are located in Los Angeles, CA; Houston, TX; Garden City, NY; Cleveland, OH; Dallas, TX; Phoenix, AZ; New York, NY; Sacramento, CA; Atlanta, GA; and Tacoma, WA.

On the other hand, natural gas buses declined as a share of all new buses from 22% in 1998 to 15% in 1999. Table 3.8 shows orders for natural-gas buses in 2001 and 2000.

Table 3.8 Natural Gas (CNG and LNG) Transit Buses in use in US Markets

	2001			2000		
	Existing	On-Order	Potential Orders	Existing	On-Order	Potential Orders
All buses	55,190	7,259	13,245	53,464	7,824	14,153
Alternative-fuel buses	5,131	1,856	2,935	3,992	1,448	3,954
Undecided			1,317			442
Natural-gas buses						
CNG	4,058	1,632	2,385	2,986	1,207	3,487
CNG / multifuel	95	45		88	41	20
LNG	575	117	465	505	129	336
LNG / multifuel	270	18		270		
Natural gas bus totals	4,998	1,812	2,850	3,849	1,377	3,843
NG as % of all AFV buses	97%	98%	97%	96%	95%	97%
NG as % of all buses	9%	25%	24%	7%	18%	28%

Source: APTA, 2001. CNG is compressed natural gas, LNG is liquefied natural gas, NG is natural gas, AFV is alternative-fuel vehicle.

CNG Bus Costs

Despite the momentum toward CNG, transit authorities provide a mixed report on the costs of buying, fuelling and maintaining CNG buses compared to diesel buses. The City of Los Angeles, for example, found that capital and operating costs for CNG buses are significantly higher than for diesel buses. Maintenance costs were much higher due in part to a higher rate of parts failures on CNG buses, indicating that the technology may not be fully mature (which in turn suggests that these costs will decline as products are improved). Paris RATP, which operates a fleet of 53 CNG buses, reports that total costs of CDG over diesel are roughly $0.25 per vehicle kilometre (RATP, 2001).

On the other hand, agencies such as Sunline Transit and Sacramento Regional Transit California, which have large numbers of CNG vehicles in their fleets, report operating costs comparable to or lower than those of diesel buses. They attribute their success with CNG to high levels of worker training, extensive experience with CNG buses and lower maintenance costs due to CNG's cleaner combustion process.

In OECD countries, the purchase price of a CNG bus is about $25,000 to $50,000 more than a diesel bus, with this cost difference declining in recent years and expected to decline further as commercial production expands. CNG buses still suffer from low production volumes resulting in high per-unit costs. High production volumes could reduce the current differential between CNG and diesel buses significantly. In developing countries, the cost difference for CNG retrofits may be much less, but the quality of the conversions is often unreliable.

Shifting from diesel to natural gas requires significant infrastructure changes. Diesel-bus depots need to be retrofitted to accommodate. Refuelling facilities have to be constructed. CNG infrastructure costs vary greatly – transit agencies report refuelling station costs of anywhere from $1 million to $5 million and bus depot modification costs from $320,000 to $15 million. These costs are influenced by at least five key factors: available space, climate, cost of materials, local regulations (e.g. regarding fire safety and building construction) and, finally, the cost of labour (NYCTRC, 2000).

In one of the more pessimistic accounts of recent CNG bus experience, the Los Angeles County Mass Transit Authority (LACMTA, 1999) recently reported the following about their CNG buses:

- Operating costs for CNG are approximately 40% higher than diesel due in part to a significantly higher rate of road repair calls.

- The incremental capital cost of procuring 200 CNG buses was approximately $14.2 million, of which $7.2 million was for bus procurement, $6.3 million for fuelling facility and $0.8 million for maintenance facility modifications.

CNG Experience in Developing Countries

Worldwide, more than nine of every ten transit buses are diesel, with which transit agencies have had more than 50 years of experience. CNG technology is perhaps diesel's closest competitor and has matured rapidly over the last decade. The trend toward natural gas in developed countries suggests that many transit agencies consider CNG buses a viable alternative to diesel buses. However, although CNG might seem an obvious alternative for transit agencies around the world seeking to meet increasingly stringent urban air-quality standards, the caveats discussed above – particularly those related to costs – should be kept in mind.

In developing countries, the purchase costs of indigenously-produced buses are likely to be much lower than in the developed world, as will be the cost differentials between CNG and diesel buses. But even with smaller differences, CNG buses may be too expensive for bus companies and agencies on very tight budgets. If developing cities have trouble affording modern, Euro-II-style diesel buses, they will have even more trouble affording CNG buses. Even advanced Euro IV diesel buses may be significantly cheaper than OEM CNG buses, depending on specification, production volumes, etc.

Additional concerns for developing countries are CNG conversion issues and availability of high-quality compressed natural gas. CNG conversions from diesel buses generally do not perform as well as original-equipment CNG buses, particularly in terms of NO_x emissions. The quality of natural gas in some countries may also be inadequate for gaseous-fuel buses. The percentage of methane in natural gas must be high and fairly constant for CNG buses to run reliably (Volvo, 1998). Finally, CNG must be handled with caution.

On the other hand, for cities that have access to low-cost CNG and do not have access to ultra-low-sulphur diesel (and there are many such cities in the developing world), CNG buses may be a good choice from an air-quality point of view.

LIQUEFIED PETROLEUM GAS

Liquid Petroleum Gas (LPG) is in some ways similar to CNG but offers some advantages in terms of performance, cost, and range. It has higher energy density than CNG and can meet transit-bus range needs with lower storage tank requirements. In many cities LPG distribution systems are well established, and LPG supplies are adequate for niche markets in the bus sector. LPG also offers good emissions performance, including low NO_x levels in engines optimised for LPG. However, until recently the LPG industry has not consistently promoted this fuel. As a result, few heavy-duty engines are commercially available, and apart from sizeable programmes in Austria,

Denmark and The Netherlands, LPG buses remain mostly in the demonstration phase. Few important obstacles confront the successful commercialisation of LPG as a motor fuel apart from the willingness of manufacturers to produce LPG vehicles.

LPG is a mixture of hydrocarbons including propane, ethane and butane, that are gases at ambient conditions but liquefy under moderate pressure. LPG is the most common alternative fuel for motor vehicles, (more than 5.5 million vehicles). LPG vehicles are common in areas where LPG supplies are abundant and prices are low, such as The Netherlands and Japan. In these situations, LPG holds some market share because it is cheaper than gasoline and users can quickly earn back the extra costs of LPG fuel-storage equipment and vehicle conversion, especially for high-kilometre drivers.

As shown in Table 3.9, the number of LPG transit buses in operation worldwide in 2000 was 1,424 in 12 European countries (WLPGA, 2001).

Table 3.9 Inventory of Liquified Petroleum Gas (LPG) Buses, 2000

Country	Number of LPG Buses
Austria	550
Belgium	2
Czech Republic	80
Denmark	250
Finland	5
France	100
Ireland	3
Italy	12
Poland	85
Spain	82
The Netherlands	200
United Kingdom	55
Total	1,424

Source: WLPGA, 2001.

Recent Programmes

Vienna

Possibly the best example of the viability of LPG as a fuel for urban transit buses comes from Vienna, where the Vienna Transport Board has been using LPG in its bus fleet for 38 years. All buses and new purchases use LPG.

Although clean-burning LPG has been shown to reduce emissions as compared to diesel (particularly CO and PM), Vienna found that NO_x emissions were greater than from diesel unless catalytic converters were used. Therefore, Vienna equipped all its LPG vehicles with three-way catalytic converters, reducing NO_x by 80% compared to diesel. The new engines meet the Euro III NO_x levels for diesel (Schodel, 1999).

With a low price for LPG in Vienna, the Vienna Transport Board indicates fuel cost savings of approximately 50% per kilometre compared to diesel.

These advantages, however, have not come without certain costs. Despite the fuel cost savings, Vienna notes that LPG bus purchase costs are 10% higher than the diesel versions and maintenance costs are 5% to 10% higher, in part due to frequent inspections of the fuel system and the catalytic converters. Thus, Vienna estimates a payback period of 13 years based on an average of 50,000 kilometres per bus per year.

Paris

The Paris Transit Agency (RATP) operates a fleet of 57 LPG buses as part of a clean-fuel evaluation programme. RATP found that the LPG buses run considerably cleaner than diesel buses using standard diesel fuel, but do not show significant advantages over diesel buses using ULSD and particulate filters. A comparison of tests for four RATP bus types – standard diesel, diesel with ULSD and a particulate filter, CNG and LPG – is shown in Figure 3.3 (RATP, 2001).

RATP estimates that LPG buses cost $0.23 per kilometre more to operate than standard diesel buses. RATP has also experienced considerable problems with local safety regulations, both for parking and operating the LPG fleet. According to current regulations, LPG buses will never be able to operate fully throughout Paris due to restrictions on use, such as in tunnels. Due to a variety of concerns, RATP recently postponed a new order for 55 LPG buses.

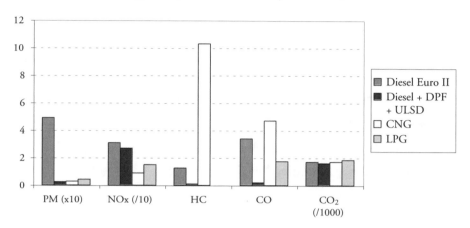

Figure 3.3 RATP Emissions Tests Results
(grams per kilometre except as noted)

Source: RATP, 2001.

Notes: As indicated by graph, actual units are: PM, tenths of a gram; NO_x, 10 grams; HC and CO, grams; CO_2, kilograms. DPF is diesel particulate filter. Hydrocarbon emissions from CNG are primarily methane, which is non-reactive (but a strong greenhouse gas).

Hyderabad

The Andhra Pradesh State Road Transport Corporation (APSRTC) has announced plans to introduce LPG buses on a pilot basis. As of Spring 2002, the Corporation and Super Gas Agency are involved in consultations to launch the project. APSRTC estimates that it would cost around Rs 2 lakh (about $4,000) to convert a single bus to run on LPG, while it would cost Rs 4 lakh ($8,000) for the same bus to run on CNG. APSRTC has no plans to use CNG buses since no CNG refuelling infrastructure exists.

Considerations in Using LPG

Some of the advantages of LPG over CNG and other options include:

■ In many countries, good industry and consumer experience in LPG storage and transport.

■ Relatively high energy density and therefore fewer compromises in fuel storage, packaging, driving range and fuel system weight than some other options.

■ A liquid at low pressures which can be carried in relatively light-weight tanks.

- In many cities, competitive in price with diesel and gasoline and able to pay back the relatively small incremental costs of an LPG vehicle (especially for conversions).

Some disadvantages include:

- At normal ambient temperatures, LPG vapours are heavier than air, meaning that leaks can lead to collections of flammable vapours in low spots. Storage and refuelling facilities must be designed appropriately.

- Poor combustion characteristics in diesel engines and therefore conversions require substantial modifications to diesel engines.

- Lower efficiency than diesel engines.

- Wide application of LPG as a motor fuel in some countries could put pressure on supplies and raise LPG prices.

- Currently, few heavy-duty LPG buses or engines are commercially available.

DIMETHYL ETHER

Use of dimethyl ether (DME) provides a way to put natural gas into a convenient liquid form as a motor fuel. It is well-suited for diesel engines and is considered a promising clean fuel by many transport experts and companies. DME has excellent combustion properties in diesel engines and good energy density. It also has no important disadvantages in terms of vehicle range or payload. To be in liquid form, DME needs to be under moderate pressure. It requires storage and dispensing hardware similar to that used for LPG. Tests in engines using DME have shown NO_x levels and particulate emissions to be very low - about half those of current (Euro III) diesel emissions standards. Production of DME has historically involved the dehydration of methanol, but these industrial processes appear unable to meet potential transportation fuel needs. No large-scale facilities of the type required have been built, and the market risks of such an investment appear substantial.

Recently, however, developments in synthesis gas conversion by companies such as Air Products and Chemicals, Inc. have lead to a commercially viable process for DME production, called the Liquid Phase DME (LPDME™)

process. As a result of this progress in DME synthesis technology, DME is being considered as a more realistic alternative to conventional diesel fuel.

A consortium including Amoco, Haldor-Topsoe and Navistar demonstrated nearly smokeless operation of diesel engines using DME in 1995. Since then, research has focussed on making DME-tolerant fuel systems, due to significant durability problems arising in part from DME's lack of lubricity – a quality that diesel fuel possesses and that diesel fuel systems have been designed to rely on (Penn State, 2001).

Interest in DME is generated, in part, because it can be produced from a wide range of feedstocks, including natural gas, biomass, agricultural and urban waste and coal. Like natural gas and methanol, DME is also a potential fuel for future fuel-cell technologies. For these reasons, in addition to DME's excellent properties as a fuel in combustion engines, the industry will probably continue a moderate level of DME research and demonstration over the next ten years.

DME Bus Technology and Emissions Performance

The unique physical properties of DME present some challenges. Apart from requiring modest pressures to maintain a liquid form, DME also has very low viscosity, leading to problems such as internal leakage in supply pumps, solenoid valves and fuel injectors. Such limitations require that significant modifications be made to conventional fuel-injection equipment to accommodate the use of DME in a diesel engine (US DOE, 2001). Operating characteristics of DME appear to be acceptable, although early experiments have used a "lubricity improver" to protect the durability of fuel injectors.

Research has shown that direct injection diesel engines fuelled with DME can achieve Euro IV and California ULEV (ultra-low-emission vehicle) exhaust emissions levels while maintaining the thermal efficiency of conventional diesels. Bench and chassis dynamometer tests indicate that DME can provide around half those of low-emissions diesel engines, without add-on emission controls, and potentially much lower with controls (Canada, 2001). The naturally low PM levels of DME buses make advanced NO_x reduction much easier than with diesel buses – for example through a "high EGR (exhaust gas recovery)" approach. DME buses with NO_x emissions control appear capable of reaching Euro V standards.

Manufacturing Process

The total world production capacity for DME currently is about 400 metric tonnes per day. It is made via fixed-bed catalytic dehydration of methanol. Although methanol dehydration is a relatively simple process, DME produced by this method will always be more costly than the methanol from which it is made. However, a new manufacturing technology is now available to reduce costs.

Amoco (BP) has taken the lead in exploring new production technologies with experienced engineering contractors. In particular, Haldor Topsoe (HT) has developed a technology for direct synthesis of DME from syngas (mixture of hydrogen plus carbon monoxide) derived from natural gas or coal. The technology is very similar to that used for the production of methanol, but there is a different catalyst in the syngas conversion step.

Haldor Topsoe developed and demonstrated, in a 50-kg-per-day pilot plant, an integrated process for the direct production of DME from synthesis gas. The HT process can produce fuel grade DME using a converter catalyst. Because of the attractiveness of this process for large-scale fuel manufacture, BP and HT have entered into an alliance for the commercial development of DME by this one-step method. The new DME technology is ready for commercialisation, which lead to the construction of large-scale, fuel-grade DME plants and further reduction in manufacturing cost. Based on their extensive experience in syngas production, methanol synthesis and DME-related pilot plant work, HT and BP Amoco have identified technology for the construction of greenfield DME plants with capacities of eight to ten thousand tons per day and consuming about 250-350 MMscfd natural gas (BP Amoco, 2001). Studies indicate that DME, if manufactured in large production plants with access to low-cost natural gas, could be made at costs somewhat less than those of methanol from comparable facilities.

Demonstration Projects

Europe

In a study partly sponsored by the IEA's *Advanced Motor Fuels* Implementing Agreement, a consortium of agencies undertook in 1999 and 2000 what may be the first effort to build (actually convert), operate and fully test a full-size DME bus. The project involved two Danish government agencies,

Swedish Volvo Bus Corporation, three bus operating companies and Statoil of Denmark (Hansen and Mikkelsen, 2001).

The converted bus was successfully operated on DME, and emissions were tested on both a bench and a chassis dynamometer. The bus achieved Euro-IV compliant emissions for all covered pollutants. A greenhouse-gas fuel-cycle analysis estimated a range of emissions for DME similar to the range for diesel and gaseous fuels such as CNG. The project also identified suitable additives for DME lubrication and odour. Finally, an analysis of large-scale plant production of DME indicated that DME fuel derived from natural gas would be competitive with diesel fuel under a range of conditions with relatively low natural-gas prices or moderately high oil prices (natural gas at $0.40/gigajoule with crude oil at $16 per barrel, or gas at $1.20 per gigajoule with oil at $22 per barrel). This of course does not provide a full picture of the relative costs of bus operation since vehicle-related costs were excluded.

A new European project called AFForHD was recently launched. It involves Volvo, TNO (a Dutch research organization), and several other European institutions. The scope is to develop a dedicated fuel injection system, fuel tank, and pump system for DME, along with a combustion-optimised engine, and integrate these into a

Volvo's DME bus is one of the first in the world (courtesy Peter Danielsson, Volvo Bus Corp.).

medium-sized truck for testing. The project will run through 2004 (Volvo *et al*, 2002).

In a separate project, a consortium of Swedish corporations and institutions is working to develop a biomass-to-DME production test facility. It involves modifying the Varnamo facility, originally built to test biomass-to-alcohol conversion. The production process involves direct gasification of feedstocks and conversion of the "synthesis gas" to DME. It is estimated that a commercial-scale bio-DME facility could produce DME at a cost of about

$0.50 per diesel-equivalent litre. The life-cycle greenhouse gas emissions from the process are expected to be very low (Volvo *et al*, 2002).

North America

Transport Canada and Natural Resources Canada recently studied safety issues regarding the use of DME as an alternative to diesel fuel, in order to develop safety guidelines for a DME fuel system. It also studied the emissions characteristics of DME systems. The project used a 5.9L Cummins engine developed to run on DME fuel.

The project recommended that some additional safety measures be used for handling DME fuel in a compression ignition system (Canada, 2001), and developed preliminary safety guidelines. A fuel system was designed to minimise the potential for DME leakage into the engine's cylinders, fuel injection pump and the atmosphere, as well as minimise the possibility of fire or explosion. DME is known to adversely affect many types of plastics and rubbers, and it was concluded that metal-to-metal seals using non-sparking metals would be the most appropriate.

In the United States, Pennsylvania State University recently converted a shuttle bus to operate on DME, to determine whether significant emissions benefits can be obtained. Conversion of a commercial diesel engine to operation on DME is not trivial, and DME presents a number of technical challenges due to its physical properties that complicate the conversion process (Penn State, 2001). The researchers investigated and characterised DME and DME diesel blends to determine the properties of both pure DME and DME mixed with diesel. They found that DME will mix completely with diesel fuel. However, a 25% DME by weight mixture had a viscosity rating well below the acceptable range for diesel fuel. When DME is mixed with diesel, viscosity drops off rapidly. The outcome from this work will be the demonstration of the fuel-conversion strategy and significant reduction in particulate and NO_x emissions from a commercial diesel vehicle.

India

Scientists in India have begun work on a joint project with BP to develop DME as an alternative clean transport fuel to help the country meet Euro-III emission norms. The Indian Institute of Petroleum (IIP), along with the Gas Authority of India Ltd. (GAIL) and the Indian Oil Corporation (IOC), recently signed a memorandum of understanding with BP (Gopolan, 1999). IOC and GAIL have taken the lead in convincing government agencies that DME is a suitable alternative fuel for transportation — as well as for use in power generation and domestic sectors. Technical and economic feasibility reports are being prepared. After establishing the commercial viability of the project, the partners will form a joint venture company to begin supplying DME to Indian power plants in 2004. The plan is to use the economies of scale of DME production for the power plants to broaden the distribution of DME as a transport fuel.

Considerations in Using DME

Benefits associated with using DME in buses include:

- A variety of possible feedstocks (including CNG and biomass).

- No major problems in transport, storage and dispensing; can utilize LPG infrastructure to a large degree.

- Simple molecular structure avoids operational problems sometimes encountered with more complex fuels in fuel distribution infrastructure and in vehicles.

- Excellent combustion characteristics in compression-ignition diesel-type engines; no major reduction in engine efficiency, range or payload.

- In experimental projects DME has produced very low NO_x and particulate levels.

Drawbacks associated with the use of DME include:

- Current price of commercial DME generally much too high to allow it to be competitive with diesel fuel; early promotional pricing may be required to build the market.

- Production of DME that could be cost-competitive with diesel fuel requires major strategic commitments and large amounts of capital, and confronts large risks.

- DME storage and distribution infrastructure would have to be built to support commercial use of DME as a motor fuel.

- No commercial DME heavy-duty engines are currently available.

- Currently available fuel-injection equipment is not suitable for DME. A system that can inject low-viscosity DME must be developed.

- DME must be stored under moderate pressures, similar to LPG.

HYBRID-ELECTRIC VEHICLES

Hybrid-electric-drive systems on transit buses are being aggressively investigated as a means of improving fuel economy and reducing emissions – especially nitrogen oxides (NO_x) and particulates (PM). They also may eventually provide improved range and reliability over conventional buses. Recent test results indicate that hybrid-bus technology is fast approaching commercial status and is becoming capable of meeting the harsh demands of transit buses.

With the rapid development and improvement of hybrid-electric-drive technology, many transit agencies are becoming interested in evaluating its potential for their fleets. Several major demonstrations are under way or have recently been completed. These have led to several new orders that will increase the number of hybrid buses in the United States from the current handful to several hundred over the next three years (375 ordered in New York City alone). The total worldwide fleet could reach the thousands within a few years.

A hybrid is defined as carrying at least two sources of motive energy on board and using electric drive to provide partial or complete drive power to the vehicle's wheels. The hybrid-electric technology is not fuel-specific, and hybrid applications have been tested using mature engine technologies and diesel, CNG and propane fuels. In a series hybrid, only the electric motor drives the wheels and the engine provides electrical energy to the motor. In a parallel hybrid, the electric motor and engine are both connected to the wheels and can both power the vehicle.

Hybrid drive offers numerous operational advantages over conventional diesel buses, such as smoother and quicker acceleration, more efficient braking, improved fuel economy and reduced emissions. Hybrids can be used on just about any duty cycle; however, regular use on high-speed express routes or hills may require design or control optimisation. Due to the complexity of the combined mechanical and electric-drive systems, maintenance requirements may be higher than for conventional buses, at least until the technology matures. Mechanical and safety retraining must also occur in light of the complexity and high-voltage components on board the bus.

Until recently, independent test data showing the emissions and fuel economy of hybrid buses were relatively scarce. A set of detailed emissions tests was recently conducted by the Northeast Advanced Vehicle Consortium (NAVC, 2000). Tests were conducted during 1999 in New York and Boston, using a transportable heavy-duty vehicle chassis dynamometer. Several different configurations of conventional and hybrid bus technologies, operating on several different fuel specifications, were tested on a variety of bus driving cycles. Overall, the results indicate that diesel hybrid-electric vehicles offer significantly reduced drive-cycle emissions relative to conventional diesel buses. However, since the hybrid buses were tested only with particulate filters and the conventional diesel buses were tested only without such filters, a direct comparison is not possible from this study.

Partial results from this study using the NYC test cycle (a rigorous test cycle with many starts and stops and a low average speed) are shown in Table 3.10. For PM, NO_x, and NMOC (non-methane organic compounds, or hydrocarbons), results are listed for eight buses: two standard diesel buses, three CNG buses and three diesel hybrid buses. The buses had different engine types, different fuel specifications (including diesel fuel with three different levels of sulphur) and different after-treatment systems. From the table, the following is apparent:

- The hybrid buses fitted with particulate filters, regardless of the type of diesel fuel used, had emissions of PM, NO_x, and hydrocarbons that were equal to or lower than CNG or diesel buses equipped only with oxidation catalysts.

- The CNG buses produced much lower PM emissions than standard diesel buses, but varied in terms of NO_x emissions. They also had the highest NMOC emissions.

- All the diesel buses (conventional and hybrid) performed significantly better when running on low-sulphur and zero-sulphur fuel than when running on standard diesel fuel. For example, conventional buses running on zero-sulphur diesel reduced PM emissions by nearly 50%.

Table 3.10 Results from NAVC study, NYC test cycle

Bus name	Engine / year	Type	Fuel	After treatment	PM g/km	NO$_x$ g/km	NMOC g/km
NovaBus RTS	DDC S-50 / 1998	Diesel	Standard diesel	Ox Catalyst	0.43	44	1
NovaBus RTS	DDC S-50 / 1998	Diesel	Zero sulphur	Ox Catalyst	0.22	45	0
New Flyer C40LF	DDC S-50G / 1999	CNG	CNG	Ox Catalyst	0.00	16	2
Orion V	DDC S-50G / 1998	CNG	CNG	Ox Catalyst	0.07	9	4
Neoplan AN44OT	Cummins L10 280G / 1998	CNG	CNG	Ox Catalyst	0.09	69	4
Nova-Allison RTS	DDC VMM 642 DI / 1998	Hybrid	Low-sulphur diesel	Johnson -M. Part. Filter	0.00	37	0
Orion-VI-LMCS	DDC S-30 / 1997/98	Hybrid	Zero sulphur	NETT Part. Filter	0.00	20	1
Orion-VI-LMCS	DDC S-30 / 1997/98	Hybrid	Standard diesel	NETT Part. Filter	0.10	25	1

Source: NAVC, 2000.

Figure 3.4 shows the tested fuel economy for different buses on the NYC test cycle. The hybrid buses all tested in the range of 55-60 litres per 100 kilometres, while the standard diesels consumed more fuel, in the 70-73 litres per 100 km range. CNG buses used the most fuel (on a diesel-equivalent basis), in the range of 75-90 litres per 100 km.

The efficiency advantage for the hybrid buses occurred despite the fact that they were heavier than the conventional diesel buses. Much of the additional energy used for accelerating this weight can be recovered via regenerative braking in the hybrid-electric vehicle, although inefficiencies in the drive motors, differential and batteries prevent the capture of all of this energy. Vehicle weight is a concern for hybrids from the standpoint of passenger-carrying capacity.

Figure 3.4 Fuel Economy Comparison, NYC Bus Test Cycle

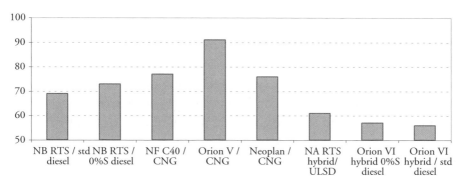

Source: NAVC, 2000.

Notes: 0%S = 0 % sulphur; ULSD = 50 ppm sulphur; std diesel = 350 ppm sulphur.

Technology Status

Hybrid-electric vehicle technology has progressed significantly in recent years, including much improved integration of components such as the auxiliary power unit (APU), energy storage system, controller and drive motor into a comprehensive system. APUs have become reliable and fuel-efficient, but more work is needed to achieve potential efficiencies and improved fuel economy while lowering emissions through reduced size and weight. The single greatest challenge facing hybrid development is battery technology. While current lead acid batteries are relatively cheap and reliable, considerable improvements in energy density, power density, life span and cost are still sought (FTA, 2000). Motors and generators have a long history of reliability, but power density and reliability are still of concern.

Some companies are also investigating "mild-hybrid" concepts that are less efficient but perform better than standard hybrids in some environments. With an integrated starter/alternator and regenerative braking, a fuel economy improvement of 7% to 8% can be achieved with a relatively small battery pack (15-20kW). This approach allows a high-torque design, particularly suited to "low engine rev" conditions (such as stop-and-go traffic)[12].

All of the components necessary to manufacture a hybrid-electric bus exist in the marketplace today, and better integration will lead to a bus that is much more efficient and has far lower emissions than today's conventional buses.

---

12 Personal communication, Peter Danielsson, Volvo Bus Corp., 2002.

In the near term, hybrids will likely take a form similar to that of a conventional bus with a diesel APU or parallel transmission, induction drive motors, conventional rear differential and lead acid batteries. Hybrid diesel buses are rapidly becoming attractive to transit agencies, due to the existing refuelling infrastructure, emission-control technologies, and the reliability of diesel engines. Hybrid technologies could achieve further emission reductions through configuration with an alternative fuel such as CNG, but this would remove compatability with current fuel systems. In the future, hybrid-electric buses may serve as the basis for a transition to fuel cells, by providing nearly all of the system components needed – with the diesel engine replaced by the fuel-cell power unit.

Demonstration Projects

A number of cities around the world are testing hybrid buses. Transit agencies that have participated in the demonstration programmes report that the benefits of hybrid buses include improved fuel economy, acceleration and handling. In-service reliability rates have reached about 70% as good as conventional diesel buses (i.e. about 30% higher failure rates).

United States

In the US, three transit agencies stand out as having extensive hybrid-drive experience to date: New York City Transit, the Los Angeles Department of Transportation and Cedar Rapids Five Seasons Transportation. Each agency operates at least five hybrid buses in revenue service and has accumulated more than 15,000 kilometres with these buses.

New York City Transit has been testing hybrid-electric-drive vehicles since the early 1990s. In 1999, it became the first transit agency in North America to demonstrate a small fleet of 40-foot hybrid transit buses in revenue service (NYCT, 2000). These Orion hybrid buses have been used to test the operational viability and economic feasibility of hybrid-drive technology for large-scale adoption by NYCT. Evidently, the positive results from the demonstrations have been enough to convince NYCT that hybrids can deliver the required performance and reduced emissions. The agency has committed to purchasing 125 more hybrid buses in 2002 and 250 in 2003. This is an important step, as it sends a signal to bus manufacturers that there is a nascent commercial market for hybrid buses. The order may also begin to push down vehicle production costs per unit, when spread over 250 buses. This may not be enough to achieve full economies of scale, but it is a good start.

In 1995, Five Seasons Transportation in Cedar Rapids, Iowa, was one of the first transit agencies in the country to begin operating electric-drive systems in regular bus service. Cedar Rapids operates five hybrid and four battery-electric buses built by Blue Bird and Northrop Grumman. The buses operate year round in demanding weather conditions, giving hybrid technologies a tough test of their performance and reliability.

The Los Angeles Department of Transportation and surrounding communities are also evaluating the use of hybrid buses as a way of helping the Los Angeles region meet ever-stricter air-quality standards. LADOT's most recent project involves testing eight hybrid buses built by Eldorado National and ISE Research. In Orange County, hybrids built by New Flyer and Solectria Corporation are in revenue service. Some of the hybrid buses will be used to demonstrate advanced technologies, including turbines and flywheels.

Europe and Latin America

The EU-sponsored Sagittaire project (EU, 2000) is running demonstrations of hybrid buses in eleven cities: Luxembourg (GD Luxembourg), Besançon (France), Alicante (Spain), Sintra (Portugal), Stavanger (Norway), Savona, Belluno and Trento (Italy), Athens (Greece), and Bruges and Leuven (represented by the regional public transportation company "De Lijn"), Belgium. In each city, the hybrid-electric bus fleet will be tested under different operational and practical conditions.

Hybrid buses are also being tested in the developing world, mainly in Latin America. The World Bank is one of the sponsors of the "Clean Air" programme, focussed on improving the air quality in Sao Paulo, Rio de Janeiro, Buenos Aires, Santiago, Mexico City and Lima. The $11-million programme will test several hybrid diesel buses in Mexico City over the next few years. A Brazilian bus company, Electra, has already begun selling a hybrid model on a semi-commercial basis, in co-operation with Marcopolo and Volvo Brazil. Three of these buses will go to Santiago, Chile, which, as part of its plan to include 3,000 clean-fuel buses in its fleet of 7,500 diesel buses by 2003, will test the three hybrid buses in a 3-month programme.

Hybrid Bus Costs

Hybrid bus life-cycle cost analysis is complicated by the fact that the technology is quite young and therefore a large body of real-world operating and maintenance costs does not yet exist. However, hybrid buses have a realistic chance of providing a net cost reduction, particularly in places with high diesel fuel prices, once the technology matures and economies of scale are reached. Until then, early adopters will have to accept a net cost increase over conventional diesel technology.

The single largest cost at present is capital acquisition (FTA, 2000). The price of a hybrid transit bus in the US has come down considerably in the last several years, from nearly one million dollars to under $400,000 today. Acquisition costs will continue to decline as volumes rise. Whether hybrids will ever cost the same as conventional diesel buses is unclear, but it is doubtful since hybrids include several additional components.

The second-largest cost in owning and operating a hybrid bus is battery replacement, which adds between $20,000 and $50,000 over the typical life of a bus. Unknown factors at this time are maintenance costs and the costs associated with potentially lower reliability levels. Maintenance costs are important to understand since maintenance typically represents a large share of total transit-bus operating expenses. Other costs include infrastructure costs, such as maintenance facilities and recharging stations.

The biggest cost-saving associated with hybrids is fuel cost. For a bus that uses close to one million litres of fuel over its service life, at a cost of $0.50 per litre, the fuel savings from hybrids can be more than one hundred thousand dollars per bus.

Ultimately, it is the fuel economy and emissions reduction potential of hybrids, coupled with their ability to run on conventional diesel fuel, that differentiates them from other options.

Considerations in Using Hybrid-Electric Buses

Issues that should be considered in the decision to use hybrid buses include:
- Hybrid-electric vehicles have significant potential for more efficient use of fossil fuels and for reductions in noise, CO_2 and other polluting emissions. They also offer the possibility of reduced refuelling

infrastructure requirements compared to all-electric vehicles or gaseous-fuel vehicles.

■ Hybrids are potentially an excellent transition technology to fuel-cell applications. In particular, they help operators gain experience with the electric drive train and ancillary components common to both hybrids and fuel-cell systems. Over the next five-to-ten years, internal-combustion-engine hybrids could be used to fully develop the electric drive train, while fuel-cell stack and other fuel-cell component technologies mature. The fuel cell could then replace the internal combustion engine in hybrid designs.

■ Although they possess great promise, hybrids are not yet sound commercial options. Even with projects moving forward in Europe and the United States, the concept of hybrid-electric buses is still relatively new, and the experience is still limited. These buses will require at least several more years of development, testing, and cost reduction before they are likely to enjoy wide-spread commercial application.

FUEL-CELL BUSES[13]

Over the past decade, the fuel cell has risen in prominence as a future option for achieving sustainable transportation. In particular, polymer electrolyte membrane (PEM) fuel cells have the potential to be an excellent power source for transportation applications, and they have emerged as a replacement for the internal-combustion engine. Like batteries, fuel cells are efficient, quiet and have no moving parts. But they also have longer driving range, high power density, and (potentially) short refuelling-time characteristics that makes them more attractive as a substitute for internal-combustion engines. Fuel-cell systems can be powered by a variety of fuels including natural gas, alcohol, gasoline or hydrogen. Vehicle emissions range from only heat and water if hydrogen is used as the fuel, to water plus CO_2 and small quantities of other regulated emissions if other fuels are used in combination with on-board hydrogen reforming (Los Alamos, 1999).

---

13   This section is based in part on interviews with various transit agencies and fuel-cell manufacturers, including Chicago Transit Agency, Vancouver Transit Agency, NYC Transit Agency, Sao Paulo Transit Agency, Ballard/XCELLSIS and International Fuel Cell Corporation.

While the fuel-cell stacks themselves are approaching maturity, many surrounding vehicle and infrastructure issues remain in early development. In particular, costs, parallel development of electric-drive systems, on-board fuel storage and refuelling infrastructure challenges are likely to impede hydrogen fuel cells from becoming a competitive propulsion system in the near term and perhaps for another decade or more. Moreover, industry has no clear development path and seems to be moving in several different directions (DeCicco, 2001).

Not surprisingly, urban transit buses are serving as an important testing ground for transport fuel-cell systems. Fuel-cell buses have already been tested by several transit agencies, and additional testing programmes planned for different cities around the world appear likely to place about 100 fuel-cell buses into operation by 2003. This includes up to 50 buses in six developing cities: Mexico City, Sao Paulo, Cairo, New Delhi, Shanghai and Beijing, as part of a five-year testing programme sponsored by the UN Development Program and the Global Environment Facility (UNDP, 2001). These tests are expected to provide valuable experience and learning to help speed technical improvements and cost reductions.

As fuel-cell vehicle technology evolves, complementary efforts will be needed to develop refuelling infrastructure and a policy environment that allows future fuel-cell buses to enter markets smoothly.

Fuel Options for Fuel-cell Systems

Although some fuel-cell systems can run on a variety of hydrogen-rich fuels like methanol, most fuel-cell vehicle research and development programmes appear to be increasingly focussed on systems that run directly on stored hydrogen. While hydrogen can be generated on board a vehicle by reforming liquid or gaseous fuels rich in hydrogen, storing hydrogen directly on board a fuel-cell vehicle greatly simplifies the system design and increases system efficiency. It also results in lower vehicle emissions.

Most studies indicate that hydrogen storage systems can be engineered to the same safety levels as conventional fuel systems. However, because hydrogen is a lightweight gas, a relatively large volume or weight is required to contain enough energy to provide the same driving range as today's vehicles. Currently, two methods of storing hydrogen are receiving the most investigation: compressed hydrogen gas in storage tanks at high pressure, and liquid hydrogen in insulated storage tanks at low temperature and pressure. Other storage methods based on metal hydrides, solid adsorbents and glass microspheres have potential advantages, but are not as developed.

The alternative to on-board storage of hydrogen is on-board fuel processing, which reforms various liquid or gaseous fuels to produce the required hydrogen immediately prior to induction into the fuel cell. The primary types of reformers currently being developed for transportation are steam reformers and partial-oxidation reformers. Designs combining elements of both types are also being investigated. On-board reformation adds significant complexity to the system (NAVC, 2000b), but it could have the advantage of using an existing fuel distribution infrastructure. The following fuels are possible candidates for on-board reforming:

- **Gasoline** contains hydrogen, and if fuel cells are designed to operate on hydrogen taken (reformed) from gasoline on board the bus, much of the existing infrastructure for fuel distribution and dispensing can be used for fuel-cell service. However, due to its complex molecular structure, gasoline is more difficult to reform than natural gas, methanol or ethanol – and is not as clean. If gasoline reformulation proves commercially viable, refineries will likely provide a "fuel-cell gasoline" that would be quite different from today's gasoline – much purer and with a narrower range of hydrocarbon types and sizes. Some companies, such as GM (working with ExxonMobil), believe gasoline makes more sense for light-duty vehicles until the commercial challenges of a hydrogen economy can be overcome (GM, 2000).

- **Methanol** reforming for fuel-cell use is simpler and inherently cleaner than reforming gasoline, although it has a lower energy density. On-board storage of methanol used to reform hydrogen, like on-board storage of hydrogen, can result in a zero-emission vehicle. On the other hand, methanol is more corrosive than gasoline and more toxic. Methanol could therefore require significantly different infrastructure than is used for gasoline service stations.

- **Ethanol** is not widely considered a strong competitor as an on-board source of hydrogen, though it could be viable for certain regions where ethanol production is high, such as Brazil. Its main strength is that it may be the best near-term renewable energy source for fuel cells. Ethanol is slightly more difficult to reform than methanol and is in some ways similar to gasoline, with similar emissions and high-temperature reformation concerns. Ethanol would be easier than methanol to make available at refuelling stations because it is relatively non-corrosive and can be distributed through existing infrastructure with only minor modifications. Its high cost is also a factor limiting its viability.

■ **Compressed natural gas** has a significant energy-density advantage over hydrogen, but this advantage does not necessarily make it worthwhile to store CNG on board a vehicle. Most current efforts appear to focus on using natural gas for off-board reformation and then storing hydrogen onboard (in tanks with compression levels up to triple that of current CNG tanks). In fact, natural gas is already the primary feedstock for manufacturing hydrogen on a commercial-scale, primarily for industrial uses. In cities with a good natural-gas distribution infrastructure, it may be cost-effective to deliver the gas to retail outlets or central bus depots. Hydrogen could then be reformed and stored on-site for use with hydrogen fuel-cell vehicles.

■ **Electrolysis** (powered by electricity) can be used to dissociate hydrogen from water, either at a central facility or at refuelling stations. Electrolysis offers a promising scenario where renewable or other non-CO_2-emitting power plants supply the electricity to produce hydrogen — yielding a near-zero-emissions system. However, electrolysis from any conventional electricity generation source brings with it that source's CO_2 emissions, as well as substantial losses in energy efficiency and potentially high costs.

If hydrogen is produced from large central plants, It can be trucked to refuelling outlets in either cryogenic-liquid or compressed-gas form. In the case of the fuel-cell bus demonstration programme in Chicago, liquid hydrogen derived from methanol was trucked to the bus garage and regasified for use on board the bus. Whether such an approach can be made practical and cost-effective on a large scale is unclear.

Environmental Characteristics of Fuel-cell Vehicles

Fuel cells are often characterised as yielding "zero emissions". When pure hydrogen is stored on board the vehicle and used directly, fuel-cell vehicles produce virtually no emissions except water. However, if emissions produced "upstream", such as from the production of hydrogen, are included, the environmental impacts of fuel cells may be substantial, depending on the source of hydrogen and the method of reformulating hydrogen-rich fuels into hydrogen.

If hydrogen is derived from electrolysis of water, powered by fossil-fired plants, upstream CO_2 emissions could be similar to or even higher than for conventional diesel buses (CFCP, 2001). If hydrogen is harvested from natural gas, the indirect emissions associated with fuel-cell buses have been estimated to be roughly half those of diesel buses (UCS, 2000).

With on-board reforming of fuels, pollutant emissions are also a concern. But these emissions can still be very low. Tests of methanol-powered fuel-cell buses with on-board reforming of methanol indicate that emissions are well below current clean-air standards, and lower than from most other bus propulsion systems. Table 3.11 shows results from recent tests in the Georgetown University demonstration programme in Washington, D.C. Methanol fuel-cell buses were compared to 1998 emissions standards and to other internal combustion engine buses (Georgetown, 2000).

Table 3.11 Criteria-pollutant Emissions from Georgetown University's Methanol-powered Fuel-cell Buses
(Grams per brake-horsepower hour)

	1998 emissions standard	DD Series 50 diesel	DD Series 50 CNG	Cummins C8.3 diesel	Cummins C8.3 CNG	94 Fuji fuel cell methanol	98 IFC fuel cell methanol
HC	1.3	0.1	0.8	0.2	0.1	0.09	0.01
CO	15.5	0.9	2.6	0.5	1.0	2.87	0.02
NO_x	4.0	4.7	1.9	4.9	2.6	0.03	0.00
PM	0.05	0.04	0.03	0.06	0.01	0.01	0.00

Source: Georgetown University 2000.
Note: DD= Detroit Diesel, IFC = International Fuel Cell.

The US Department of Transportation compared representative emissions of fuel-cell and internal-combustion-engine vehicles using various fuels (FTA, 2000). These are shown in Figure 3.5, along with the 1998 US standards in place when the tests were performed. The fuel-cell data are based upon vendor projections derived from experience in the use of fuel cells as stationary power plants. The fuel cell emits trace amounts of hydrocarbons and NO_x, very little carbon monoxide and no particulate matter.

Figure 3.5 Representative Emissions of Fuel Cell and other Bus Technologies

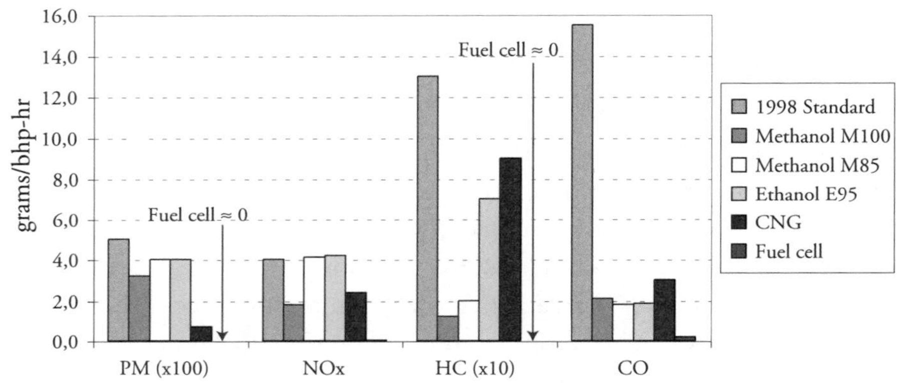

Source: FTA, 2000.

Note: as indicated by the figure, actual units for PM are one one-hundredth of a gram; for HC, one-tenth of a gram.

In a study by Levelton (1999) for the Canadian government, greenhouse gas emissions from buses were assessed for several different propulsion technologies and fuels. As shown in Figure 3.6, fuel-cell buses can produce lower life-cycle (or "fuel-cycle") emissions than diesel buses, but that depends on the feedstock and upstream processes used to produce hydrogen. The figure includes three types of fuel-cell bus: one running on methanol with on-board reforming of hydrogen, and two with off-board production of hydrogen: one from natural gas (H_2NG) and one from electricity (H_2E). Due in part to the efficiency losses from on-board reforming, the methanol bus is estimated to produce nearly as much fuel-cycle CO_2-equivalent emissions as diesel buses. The other two fuel-cell bus types do better, providing about a 30% reduction compared to diesel. For the bus running on hydrogen produced from electricity (through electrolysis), this electricity is assumed to come from an average mix of Canadian power plants, including those powered by nuclear, hydro, coal and natural gas. With electricity produced only by renewables or nuclear power (not shown), the net CO_2-equivalent emissions this fuel cell would be near zero.

Figure 3.6 Fuel-Cycle CO_2-Equivalent Emissions for City Transit Buses
(grams/mile)

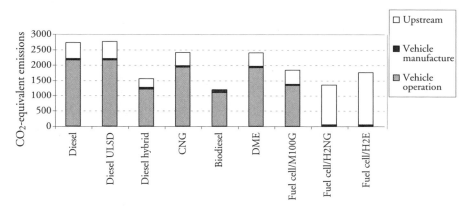

Source: Levelton, 1999.

Notes: Fuel cell/M100NG is fuel-cell-powered by methanol-100 from natural gas; Fuel cell/H2NG is powered by hydrogen from natural gas; Fuel cell/H2E is powered by hydrogen from electricity, with an average generating mix for Canada. For biodiesel, upstream CO_2 = -710, vehicle use CO_2 = 2153. The (negative) upstream value has been added to the vehicle use to show the overall total.

It is also worth noting the study's emissions estimates for other fuels. Buses running on pure biodiesel would provide the greatest reductions in greenhouse emissions, followed by hybrid-electric buses running on diesel. CNG and DME provide less than a 10% reduction compared to standard diesel. Buses running on ultra-low-sulphur diesel (ULSD) produce about 1.5% more greenhouse emissions than regular diesel buses, mainly due to increased energy requirements to produce the fuel.

Fuel-cell Applications in The Urban Transit Bus

The various characteristics of the urban transit bus market make it a good test bed for introducing fuel-cell technologies. One advantage to developing fuel cells for the transit bus sector is the central fuelling infrastructure. Since transit buses are typically centrally refuelled, new refuelling infrastructure would only be needed at bus depots. Additionally, in most developed cities buses are refuelled and maintained by a skilled, dedicated staff that can be trained to safely dispense hydrogen. However, the number of bus companies in the developing world prepared to undertake the challenge of maintaining a fuel-cell bus fleet remains to be seen.

Another advantage is that a large transit vehicle offers good "packaging" options for fuel-cell systems, including hydrogen storage. Buses have more space than smaller vehicles to accommodate the fuel cell and the compressed-hydrogen tanks.

Finally, many municipal transit agencies are under pressure to reduce the environmental and societal impact of their vehicles. Fuel-cell systems, though expensive, are attractive, high-profile options for addressing urban environmental problems like air pollution, and noise.

On the other hand, the transit bus market is probably too small to support full commercialisation of fuel cells on its own. Fuel-cell commercialisation appears increasingly likely to be driven by sales in stationary applications, which could be several orders of magnitude greater than for buses. Even commercialisation of transport-specific components of fuel-cell systems may need to rely on sales in the much larger truck market. The main area where substantial sales of fuel-cell buses might bring down costs is in the assembly of complete systems for buses.

Barriers to Commercialisation

Despite the environmental reasons for using fuel cells and the on-going development of fuel-cell technologies, a number of hurdles could slow commercialisation:

- **Development and testing.** Much development work is still needed for fuel-cell systems and ancillary components. Component size and weight reductions are needed, as well as rapid start-up, and improved temperature control, and improved reliability.

- **Refuelling infrastructure.** Beyond the vehicle components, one of the biggest hurdles could be refuelling infrastructure, depending upon the type of fuel chosen. New infrastructure systems will be necessary for generating hydrogen gas and for delivering hydrogen to refuelling stations.

- **On-board hydrogen storage.** Advancements in storage technology could have a big impact in accelerating the acceptance and commercialisation of fuel-cell vehicles. Hydrogen gas storage systems need to be lighter and highly reliable.

- **Achieving scale economies.** Development of large-scale low-cost production systems is needed, particularly in terms of standardising platforms for integration of the hydrogen fuel-cell stack, electro-drive components, batteries, and on-board gas storage and delivery systems.

- **Transit-agency experience.** Lack of experience with fuel-cell buses as well as with transporting, handling and storing gaseous fuels will take time and limited-scale testing to overcome.

- **Codes and standards.** Standards for hydrogen storage and transportation need significant work before there can be any significant market share for fuel cells. In some cases current restrictions will need to be removed. These include parking and travel restrictions on hydrogen-fuelled vehicles and restrictions on distribution and handling of gaseous fuels. But to achieve the needed changes in standards, development of adequate safety measures will be needed.

Perhaps the greatest barrier is cost. Fuel-cell bus manufacturing costs are very high. For example, the Ballard/Xcellsis Phase 5 models currently being tested in the US and Europe are estimated to cost over one million dollars per bus, about four times the price of a standard diesel bus. These costs are high, in part, because of the R&D costs imbedded in each vehicle and the fact that they are still manufactured as "one-off" items.

Some experts believe that after some additional technological refinements, perhaps even after the current round of demonstrations and evaluations, the fuel-cell bus industry will be ready to begin production on a semi-commercial basis. The UNDP/GEF project described below has set a target to reduce production costs by about half, to half a million dollars per bus or less, through the technology learning that occurs in that project[14]. If this is achieved, perhaps in conjunction with scaled-up production, fuel-cell buses may begin to compete with other advanced technologies and clean-fuel buses in markets demanding very clean vehicles. Whether fuel-cell bus prices will ever be competitive with conventional diesel buses or even CNG buses is, however, still an open question.

---

14   Richard Hosier, UNDP fuel cell bus project manager, personal communication.

On-Road Demonstrations of Fuel-cell Buses

Although a number of fuel-cell manufacturers are heavily involved in the research and development of applications for the transportation sector, Ballard Power Systems has perhaps been the most aggressive in working with auto companies to produce prototype bus models for on-road testing. One of the first demonstration vehicles using modern fuel-cell technology was a 32-foot bus built by Ballard in 1993, effectively emerging as "Phase 1" of their on-going demonstration programme. The programme is currently entering "Phase 5" in the US and Europe. Chicago and Vancouver each demonstrated three Ballard/Xcellsis "Phase 3" fuel-cell buses over a two-year period ending in September 2000. The "Phase 4" is currently undergoing road testing by Sunline Transit Agency in Palm Springs, California (Xcellsis, 2001).

The Xcellsis Phase 4 fuel-cell bus features a 205-kilowatt hydrogen-powered fuel-cell stack. Due to improvements in efficiency and a lighter fuel cell, this bus is able to carry 75 passengers 550 kilometres. The Phase 4 bus is about 10% lighter than the Phase 3 (14,376 kg v. 15,646 kg), with better acceleration, fewer parts and improved power density – all of which result in lower capital and operating costs. Maintenance and repair costs are expected to be about one-tenth of Phase 3 engines (Sunline, 2001).

In Phase 5 of the programme, Daimler Chrysler's subsidiary EvoBus will deliver 30 "Citaro" fuel-cell buses with Ballard/Xcellsis fuel-cell systems to European bus operators, beginning in 2002. These buses will operate in nine European cities: Amsterdam, Barcelona, Hamburg, Stuttgart, London, Luxembourg, Porto, Stockholm and Reykjavik. Other cities are expected to participate after 2002. The 12-metre long, low-floor Citaro is a regular-service transit bus. Depending on operating conditions it will have an operating range of 200 to 250 kilometres and will be able to accommodate up to 70 passengers. The maximum speed is approximately 80 kilometres per hour. The fuel-cell unit has an output of more than 200 kilowatts. Compressed-hydrogen storage tanks are installed on the roof.

Other notable projects include:

■ **Georgetown University's** fuel-cell-powered transit bus was introduced in May 1998. The bus uses a 100 kilowatt phosphoric acid fuel-cell engine from International Fuel Cells. It is methanol-fuelled and has a range of 550 kilometres. In March 2000, Georgetown University unveiled its second 12-metre fuel-cell-powered transit bus on campus, made possible through a programme with the Federal Transit Administration. The bus has a Novabus RTS platform, a Lockheed Martin Control Systems electric drive, a vehicle system controller by Booz-Allen and Hamilton and a 100kW PEM fuel cell developed by Ballard/Xcellsis.

- **Siemans/MAN's** 12-metre, low-floor transit bus powered by a 120kW 400V Siemens/KWU PEM fuel cell. Hydrogen stored on the roof of the bus has a total volume of 1548 litres, and lasts over 250 kilometres. Following more testing, the bus was used in public transit service in 2000 in the cities of Nurnberg and Erlangen. MAN is planning a second-generation of liquid-hydrogen- powered buses, to be demonstrated in Berlin, Lisbon and Copenhagen.

- **Neoplan's** first fuel-cell bus was launched in October 1999. The eight-metre bus is powered by a 50kW DeNora PEM fuel cell, with a battery providing auxiliary power, for a total power capability of 150kW. It is fuelled with compressed hydrogen. Neoplan and Proton Motor Fuel Cell GmbH displayed a hybrid PEM fuel-cell bus at Munich's "Fuel-cell Day" in May 2000. The bus contains a 400V, 80kW PEM fuel-cell system. Extra energy for acceleration and hill climbing is provided by a 100kW flywheel system.

- **Renault V.I. and Iveco's** began road testing a 60kW hydrogen fuel-cell bus in Torino, Italy, in June 2001. The project is financed by the private and public sectors, and depending on results, might lead to the purchase of more zero-emission vehicles during the latter half of the decade.

- **Thor Industries** plans to build commercially viable fuel-cell buses in an alliance with International Fuel Cells (IFC) and ISE Research. The first bus was built in 2001. Thor has exclusive rights for use of IFC's fuel cells in the complete drive system, called Thunder Power, for all North American mid-sized buses. ISE Research will provide its hybrid system and perform the fuel-cells systems integration. The US Department of Transportation has committed $740,000 to Thunder Power towards the development of a 30-foot hydrogen fuel-cell transit bus.

Fuel-Cell Buses in Developing Countries

As part of its strategy to introduce clean technologies and reduce greenhouse gas emissions in developing nations, the Global Environment Facility (GEF) has given a green light to the use of fuel-cell buses in a demonstration project in five countries.

Between 2002 and 2003, GEF plans to pay the incremental costs for the operation of 40-50 fuel-cell buses in Sao Paulo, Mexico City, New Delhi, Cairo, Beijing and Shanghai, pending each country's approval of the project. Brazil is slated to be the first to use the fuel-cell buses. The GEF, a multilateral trust fund which works through the United Nations Development Program (UNDP), the UN Environment Program (UNEP) and the World Bank, will contribute $60 million of the $130 million projected cost. The five countries will pick up remaining costs, with a small amount contributed by private industry.

Although the initial cost of fuel-cell buses is substantial, the 33-member GEF is considering the eventual commercialisation of the technology, which they project to occur between 2007 and 2010. Each country will need its own manufacturing infrastructure to increase production. Once this happens, the costs per bus will hopefully fall, through learning, scale economies, and the low costs associated with production in developing countries (UNDP, 2001, Hosier, 2000).

In Sao Paulo, Brazil, EMTU/SP (Empresa Metropolitana de Transportes Urbanos de Sao Paulo) will participate in the UNDP/GEF fuel-cell project, which is one to two years behind schedule, largely due to financing delays. EMTU is aware that the fuel-cell demonstration project is not, in itself, going to be commercially viable. Their motivation for participating in this early stage includes:

- Improving the awareness of fuel-cell technology and associated benefits— with a secondary rationale of demonstrating to the Sao Paulo public that the municipal government is taking serious steps to mitigate local air-pollution problems.

- Sharing in the emissions benefits while advancing the technology.

- Building capacity to use hydrogen. To this end, the project will remain in EMTU/public-sector hands for training and learning; local universities will be involved in testing and R&D.

- As the largest bus manufacturer in the world, Brazil would like to create a foothold in a future fuel-cell market.

- As a major producer of ethanol from sugar cane, Brazil is very interested in developing the ethanol-hydrogen cycle.

CHAPTER SUMMARY: MOVING UP THE TECHNOLOGY LADDER

A range of engine technologies and fuels has been reviewed that can provide dramatic reductions in bus emissions and, in some cases, reductions in greenhouse-gas emissions or consumption of fossil fuels. Among the most cost-effective options are simply maintaining existing buses to a higher standard and making incremental improvements in diesel buses through improved engine design, emission control, and fuel quality. At the other extreme, new technologies such as hybrid-electric and fuel-cell propulsion systems offer very clean buses for the future, but currently are still under development and can be very expensive. Somewhere in-between lie alternative fuels such as CNG, LPG, and DME – non-petroleum, clean fuels that are neither inexpensive nor necessarily easy to establish, but that could provide an interim solution for some cities.

Despite the effort to develop alternative fuels, heavy-duty engine manufacturers continue to focus much of their effort on improving diesel engines for large buses, with the primary goal of meeting future emissions standards of OECD countries. Diesel buses still comprise over 90% of the US transit bus fleet, and a similar share in Europe. CNG buses represent by far the most popular alternative fuel, and have grown in number in the US from about 100 in 1992 to over 4 000. But with a commitment by the NY City Transit agency to purchase 350 hybrid-electric buses over the next three years, market introduction of this advanced technology has arguably begun. Fuel-cell buses are now being tested (or tests are planned) in small quantities (typically 2 or 3) in about 15 cities in North America and Europe.

Table 3.12 summarises the IEA's estimates of costs associated with different options. Clearly, steps up this cost "ladder" do not come cheaply, and bus companies that currently can barely afford to by new, locally made buses that might cost $50 to $75 thousand are not in a position to consider advanced technologies costing hundreds of thousands or even millions of dollars. They may even lack the resources to purchase basic OECD-style diesel buses meeting Euro-II standards. Similarly, the cost of gaseous-fuel buses, and developing a fuel distribution and refuelling infrastructure to support their use, may be daunting. The box on the following page provides one scenario of how

Table 3.12 Bus Technology Cost Estimates
($ thousands)

Category	Bus purchase cost	Other costs
Small, new or second-hand bus seating 20-40, often with truck chassis	10-40	
Large, modern-style diesel bus that can carry up to 100 passengers, produced by indigenous companies or low-cost import	40-75	
Diesel bus meeting Euro II, produced for (or in) developing countries by international bus companies	100-150	Some retraining and possibly higher spare parts and equipment costs
Standard OECD Euro II diesel bus sold in Europe or US[a]	175-350	
Diesel with advanced emissions controls meeting Euro III or better	5-10 *more* than comparable diesel bus	If low sulphur diesel, up to $0.05 per litre higher fuel cost (for small or imported batches)
CNG, LPG buses	25-50 *more* than comparable diesel bus (less in developing countries)	Refuelling infrastructure costs could be up to several million dollars per city
Hybrid-electric buses (on a limited production basis)	75-150 *more* than comparable diesel bus	Potentially significant costs for retraining, maintenance and spare parts
Fuel-cell buses (on a limited production basis)	Up to one million dollars *more* than comparable diesel buses, even in LDCs at this time	Possibly millions of dollars per city for hydrogen refuelling infrastructure and other support-system costs

Source: IEA data.

a. Note that this range of prices includes transit buses in both Europe and North America. Buses in Europe are generally less expensive than in North America, with the prices in Europe for non-articulated buses generally below $275,000.

companies might be able, over time, to move up the "technology ladder". An important part of this process is learning and gaining the capability to handle more complex technologies and systems. But it is also dependant on money; unless bus systems are improved, and each bus generates considerable revenue, it is unlikely that companies will be able to move very far up this ladder.

Stepping up the Technology Ladder

The following are some of the possible steps up the bus "technology ladder", in approximate order of cost and complexity:

- **Basic bus maintenance:** many bus companies do not maintain their existing buses well, leading to high emissions and low fuel economy. Inspection and maintenance systems could be strengthened quite cheaply, although strong enforcement is needed. Lower diesel fuel sulphur levels can also help, and if moderately low-sulphur diesel is available (<1000 ppm), low-cost oxidation catalysts could be added to many existing buses to reduce CO and HC emissions, and to a lesser extent PM emissions.

- **Clean technology buses:** standard buses built for OECD countries are far cleaner than many buses built in developing countries. OECD-calibre buses built in the countries that will use them may be a lower-cost alternative and help develop the vehicle manufacturing industries in each country. Improvements should begin with better engines.

- **Clean diesel fuel:** ultra-low-sulphur diesel, or even blends of standard diesel with 10% water, can reduce bus emissions substantially. Combined with advanced emissions control systems (that require low-sulphur fuels), these systems can result in diesel buses with emissions comparable to most alternative fuels and relatively low vehicle cost.

- **Alternative fuels:** the gaseous fuels (CNG, LPG, and DME) discussed in this chapter offer the possibility of "inherently" clean bus travel. For optimal performance, engines should be used that are designed to run on these fuels rather than converted from diesel. The viability of different fuels in different cities depends in part on fuel availability and fuel supply infrastructure. Installation of refuelling infrastructure can be difficult and costly, and companies must be trained in the handling and use of gaseous fuels.

- **Hybrid electric:** while providing something close to an inherently clean diesel technology, hybrid-electric propulsion is still being tested, and its costs may be out of reach for many cities for years to come. But it is increasingly seen as part of the transition to fuel cells since it employs the same type of electric-drive system, and because this technology appears likely to be commercialised much sooner.

- **Fuel cells:** once experience is gained with electric-drive systems, and if possible with gaseous-fuel vehicles and refuelling systems, cities should be more prepared to deal with operating and maintaining fuel-cell buses. This is still a big step, since fuel-cell systems are complex. If buses with on-board reforming are introduced then the complexity level and importance of good maintenance practice will be even greater. Cities just beginning to work with fuel cells and hydrogen fuel systems may find it useful to partner with cities that have already gained experience in these areas, in order to speed the learning and competence-building process.

4

BUS SYSTEM DEVELOPMENT: SIX CASE STUDIES

The IEA worked with cities around the world that are attempting to develop better bus systems (not those *already* possessing improved systems, discussed elsewhere in the report). We attempted to understand the current transportation situation in these cities, their goals for transport and, in particular, transit-related improvements, and what obstacles they face. This chapter presents case studies of six cities. For each city, a discussion is presented of the present economic and transport situation, trends and issues, the present bus system characteristics, recent initiatives in transport in general and those related to buses and steps that could be taken to improve transit.

In addition, transport data are presented for each city, with as much of an "ASIF" matrix as possible – that is, data on travel Activity, modal Structure, energy Intensity, and Fuel choice, as well as fuel-related factors such as CO_2 emissions per litre and pollutant emissions per kilometre of travel[15]. The types of data available vary widely. Overall, however, the data for these cities indicate that while buses account for a relatively small part of transport emissions, they account for a much larger share of passenger travel. Further expanding and enhancing bus systems, with commensurate increases in ridership, could provide substantial benefits.

The six case studies suggest that improved bus transit systems could play a much bigger role in moving people and improving city life – and that citizens and officials are beginning to understand this potential. All these cities would benefit from greater international assistance in bringing their projects to fruition.

SURABAYA, INDONESIA

Surabaya, located on the north coast of Java in Indonesia's East Java province, is the second-largest city in Indonesia. Though it is much smaller than Jakarta (2.5 million v. nearly 10 million), the land area is also much smaller

---

15   See, for example, Schipper et al, 2000, for a discussion of the ASIF approach to data collection and analysis.

(about half), and there is far less roadway capacity, especially major arterials and highways. Surabaya is typical of the numerous large regional cities in Indonesia.

Surabaya has experienced rapid economic and transport growth in the past 10 years. Car ownership continues to grow despite the economic crisis of 1997. Traffic congestion and associated problems are now major concerns of the citizens and local government. A major World Bank study completed in 1998 predicts rapidly worsening congestion over coming years, with a declining share of public transit, from 35% in 1998 to 23% of all motorised trips in 2010. Local officials feel that this is a critical time for Surabaya to determine its transport future and political support for improving public transport is growing. Since Surabaya is not the National Capital, the local government has strong control over transport planning. But many agencies are involved and need to co-ordinate their activities.

Current Transport System

While traffic and congestion have increased, few major roadway projects have been undertaken in Surabaya in recent years. This infrastructural "status quo" may actually provide opportunities to show the citizens of Surabaya how the existing infrastructure can be used more efficiently. In a sense Surabaya is less "far gone" than the capital city, Jakarta – less car dependent and less committed to roadway expansion as a solution to transport problems.

The World Bank projects that with "business as usual" travel growth, traffic congestion in Surabaya will continue to worsen and by 2010 more than half of main roads will be operating at or above capacity, with average vehicle speeds less than 10 kilometres per hour (Dorsch et al, 1998).

A key aspect to traffic in Surabaya is the mix of vehicle types (Table 4.1). *Becaks* (non-motorised three-wheelers) still ply major thoroughfares. Surabaya also has a large number of motorcycles and mopeds. There are more than three times as many motorised two-wheelers as cars. The city also has ten times more minibuses and vans (*angkots*) than full-size buses (about 5000 v. 500).

Given an interest in increasing the travel share of large buses, an important question is how many motorcyclists and moped riders would switch to bus ridership as service improves. Surveys indicate a willingness to pay for increased service quality, with factors such as transit reliability, comfort

Table 4.1 Licensed Vehicles in Surabaya

Vehicle type	Number	Average passenger capacity	Avg. annual utilisation (km)	Total annual travel (million km)	Fuel economy (km/l)
Cars/light trucks	175,000	5	N/A	N/A	8 – 10
Buses	470	50-60 seated; up to 100 including standing	60,000	18 (based on 300 buses)	2 - 3.5
Angkots (vans)	5,000	12-15	60,000	300	6 – 8
Motorised 2-wheelers	670,000	2-3	N/A	N/A	40
Becaks (non-motorised 3 wheelers)	40,000	2-3	N/A	N/A	N/A

Source: Surabaya Sustainable Urban Transport Project, "Transport Planning and Physical Improvements", 2000; Surabaya in Figures 1999.

(especially during the wet season) and security rated more important than fare. As long as public transit does not offer an attractive alternative to motorcycles it will continue to lose modal share (since that is the largest group). As incomes rise, many motorcycle users will eventually become car users, which will compound the traffic problem and make it harder to solve.

Transport is the main source of air pollution in Surabaya. In 1992 transport was responsible for more than 95% of carbon monoxide emissions, 71% of hydrocarbons, 33% of NO_x, and was a major source of particulates and lead. This contribution has no doubt increased since 1992 due to the worsening traffic conditions, increased motorisation, and a shift of much industry to peripheral areas. Morbidity data for Surabaya (Table 4.2) shows that respiratory illness is a serious health problem.

Current Bus System

The Surabaya city government, in co-operation with Germany's technical co-operation agency GTZ, has developed an initiative to improve the city's transport system, with a focus on improving bus transit services (SUTP, 2002).

Table 4.2 Illness Breakdown by Age Group

Age group	Most common illness	Total	%
0 – 28 days	Acute infections in the upper respiratory tract	2,324	46.3
28 days – 1 year	Acute infections in the upper respiratory tract	41,923	47.4
1 – 4 years	Acute infections in the upper respiratory tract	68,182	41.9
> 60 years	Muscle and tissue illness	54,486	23.4

Source: Profil Kesehatan Kota, Surabaya Tahun 2001.

Note: most common recorded illnesses at community health centres in Surabaya in 2000 according to age group.

This effort has provided considerable information on the current bus system and identified an approach to improving it.

Currently fewer than 500 buses operate on about 20 fixed bus routes around the city. A recent review of bus service revealed that only about half these routes provide regular bus service (at least every 20 minutes). There are also nearly 60 *angkot* (van) routes. Most of the bus routes have a north-south axis while most of the *angkot* routes run east-west.

Buses operate on fixed routes, with many different companies operating buses on the same routes. The lack of any effective route planning and the failure of the licensing system to impose any service requirements on operators have contributed to the poor service. Since buses are regulated individually, rather than at the route level, no individual operator has any responsibility for the overall level of service on the route. Buses are required only to operate on the route; not to provide any particular level of service or be maintained at a minimum level. There are no requirements for bus frequency or comfort. Fares are regulated but not at a level sufficient to cover many operators' costs. Revenues are hampered by low bus speeds and long queues and waiting times in bus terminals. Passengers have none of the benefits of an integrated system, such as free transfers or convenient transfer points.

Buses are required to begin and end their routes at bus terminals. There are relatively few terminals for large buses. The terminals are intended to be major transfer points for many routes so that economies of scale are created. However, this large scale contributes to poor conditions at terminals. They tend to be chaotic, dirty, and unsafe. Inadequate bus bays result in buses from different routes sharing lanes; this, in turn, causes long delays. A recent GTZ report (Neilson, 2000) makes the following observations:

"Private buses are rented to individual drivers on a daily basis under the 'setoran' system. No scheduling of these buses is done and as a result on all routes, other than the exclusive Damri [public bus company] routes, the drivers simply drive to the terminus at the start of the day (or well before it) and take their place in the queue for departure. Since there is apparently no avoiding the terminus, it is clearly in an individual driver's interest to wait at the terminus for a longer rather than shorter period as he can a) get more passengers at the terminus and b) more passengers at the bus stops on route due to the longer gap between his bus and the one in front. Departure times from termini are determined partly by the driver and partly by 'co-ordinators' providing informal terminus control. Although in theory the control card, which each bus must carry, should contain the schedule for that specific bus, in practice this is not done."

Figure 4.1 Bus Service Frequency on Different Routes
(by number of terminal departures per hour)

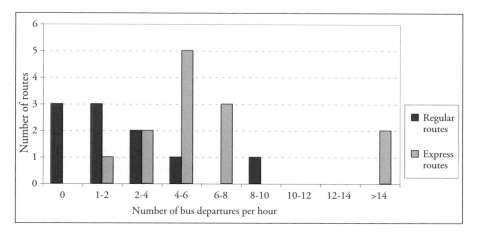

The same report provides data on bus route coverage and average "headway" times (times between bus departures from the terminal). Results from a survey of bus departures from Surabaya's main bus terminal during the peak morning period are reproduced in Figure 4.1, and the average time between bus arrivals at a stop on one route is shown in Figure 4.2.

Figure 4.2 Headways on One of the Better-served Routes
(Minutes)

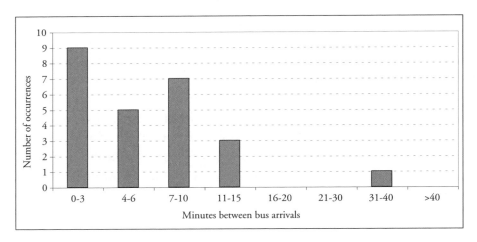

Assuming a goal of one terminal departure every five minutes, it would be necessary to have 12 buses depart per hour. Only one bus route achieved this level. Most routes had fewer than one departure every 10 minutes, and three routes provided no bus service at all, at least during the survey period. On one of the "better-served" routes, closer analysis (Figure 4.2) reveals a different story: although more than a third of departures were within three minutes of the previous one, there were four that were more than 10 minutes and one that was more than 30 minutes relative to the previous departure.

Damri, the public bus operator, is the dominant bus operator in Surabaya. Its 288 buses represent about 60% of the total urban bus fleet[16]. The newest batch of 20 Damri buses is three years old. The average is nine years old. Private sector operators use even older buses, with most retired from inter-city services. All buses use high-sulphur diesel fuel and typically emit high levels of particulates and black smoke. With declining profitability and increasing costs due to deteriorating traffic conditions, as well as uncertainty regarding the future regulatory environment, operators do not invest much in new buses. Typical bus capacities are 100 passengers including standing room. Average peak loads on main routes in early 2000, based on GTZ surveys, were 78, so buses were fairly full but not overcrowded.

---

16   Damri's 288 buses account for 60% of the total fleet of large buses in Surabaya. The largest private operator has only 15 buses; only four operators have more than 10 buses while the average fleet size is six.

Most of Damri's buses are Mercedes (about 270) and some are Hino (about 20). Most of the private large city bus fleet is Hino. All are imported and assembled in Indonesia. The cost of a full size bus is approximately Rp. 625 million (about $75,000) for an air-conditioned bus and less than Rp. 500 million ($60,000) for a non-air conditioned bus.

Recent Initiatives

The city's effort to develop an improved, integrated transit system features support for non-motorised transport, cleaner fuels, and traffic management to limit the use of private motor vehicles. The centrepiece is a planned bus demonstration project on a new bus route along the major north-south corridor within the city. Other components of the plan include:

- Promotion of bike use and walking, with improved facilities for pedicabs.

- Improved facilities and safety for pedestrians.

- A strategy for improving traffic safety.

- A strategy for reducing traffic in residential and mixed districts.

- Improved vehicle inspection and maintenance programmes.

- Introduction of unleaded gasoline.

- CNG conversions for some vehicles.

- Air-quality monitoring and management.

- Adjustments to fuel taxes.

- Additional parking management efforts.

- Institutional reforms, such as for bus licensing.

- A commission with representatives from relevant government authorities to evaluate administration in the transport and environment sectors.

- Raising public awareness of the need for a sustainable urban transport system.

Planned Pilot Bus Project

Within this broad programme, a priority is the implementation of the pilot bus project. The following specific elements were recommended by GTZ, technical supporters of the project:

- A new route licensing system whereby the government would set service criteria; Service is then awarded on a competitive and transparent tender basis to private operators, with one operator per route.

- Deregulation of the complicated and inflexible regulatory system.

- Physical improvements to bus stops and shelters, footpaths and bus terminals.

- A priority busway along the demonstration route, covering the most congested 5.6 kilometre portion of the route.

- An additional lane in the corridor for non-motorised vehicles.

The recommended corridor runs north-south through the heart of the city.

Much of the preparatory work for the pilot bus project has already been completed, and the foundations appear to be in place: strong political support, identification of the route, the main elements of the licensing and tendering scheme, and identification of physical improvements needed to the corridor. The project has the support of the mayor of Surabaya, the adjoining Regent of Sidoarjo, the central government Directorate General of Land Transport, the public transport operators association, and the City Planning Board. The Road Traffic Office has not expressed opposition, but so far has not acted to implement the programme. If the project is successful, the national government in Jakarta would like it to be a model for the nation. The total cost of the project is estimated to be Rp. 458 million (about $50,000), which includes modest infrastructure improvements.

How the Pilot Project Could be Strengthened

One concern about the project is that its scale, and the number of buses involved, is small. Therefore it may be difficult to attract large and/or international bus operators, who have the resources to provide relatively modern buses. However, there are advantages to involving local operators and giving them a stake in the new system. GTZ has demonstrated that the route would be financially viable for small operators even with the purchase of new buses. Since the age of the buses is one of the conditions of the tender, there is no danger that old buses would be used on the pilot route.

Nevertheless, in order to generate interest in the tender on the part of all types of operators, even while requiring the acquisition of new, clean buses, it may make sense to offer them assistance with the incremental costs of these buses over what is normally bought. This could include encouraging the development of co-operative bidding arrangements among small operators, or seeking outside funding to help pay for certain incremental costs, such as for Euro-II compliant rather than "Euro-O" buses.

The pilot project could also be strengthened by upgrading the physical improvements planned along the bus route, such as bus stop design, better access for pedestrians and bicycles, and by deploying bus system technologies such as bus tracking systems with real-time schedule displays. Technical assistance from cities that have successfully implemented bus rapid transit systems would also help identify steps to ensure that Surabaya develops a "best-practice" system. Similarly, it would be helpful for Surabaya officials to see, first-hand, world-class BRT systems such as in Bogota.

The pilot project is a promising opportunity to promote sustainable transport in a typical large Indonesian city. Surabaya is not yet a "lost cause" for public transit, but action is needed now to arrest its declining importance. The bus project is well- conceived and has considerable stakeholder support, but still would benefit from additional resources and technical assistance. Finally, the institutional, regulatory and planning changes that are to be implemented as part of the pilot route are a critical component; without these, the impact on transit service just from provision of improved physical facilities would likely have only a minor and unsustainable impact.

DHAKA, BANGLADESH

Metropolitan Dhaka is the largest and most industrialised city in Bangladesh, and its administrative, commercial, and cultural capital. The population of Dhaka was eight million in 1995 and is projected to reach 16 million by 2015, making it the seventh largest city in the world. Between 1960 and 1990 the population grew an average of eight percent per year. With a seven percent share of the country's population, Dhaka contributes about 13% to the national GDP. But despite its importance in the national economy, the city suffers from acute deficiencies in infrastructure, resulting in a widening gap between supply and demand for sector services. Recognising the extent of Dhaka's transport problems, the national government commissioned the Dhaka Integrated Transport Study (DITS) in 1994. Subsequent studies have updated some of the findings and data from this study, providing a picture of the current transport system.

Current Transport System

Dhaka is characterised by chronic traffic congestion, inadequate traffic management, rapidly worsening air quality, and poor co-ordination among agencies trying to address these problems. It may be the only city of its size without any centrally organised, scheduled bus or other mass transport system. Traffic problems have reached crisis proportions, with delays tripling between 1998 and 2001. Several recent public campaigns have called for urgent solutions. The addition of another eight million people over the next 20 years will no-doubt make conditions even more difficult.

Travel modes in Dhaka are in certain respects unique among large Asian cities. Almost 40% of the nine million weekday trips are on foot; 30% are by non-motorised cycle-rickshaw; eight percent are by motorised three-wheel auto-rickshaw; four percent by bus; one percent by private car; and the remaining 17% are by government provided transport, school bus, and train. Thus, more than two-thirds of trips are non-motorised. Dhaka probably has the most cycle rickshaws in the world, well over 100,000. The high dependence on walking and cycle rickshaw and low use of buses, in a city of eight million people with an urban area of 2,000 square kilometres, are symptoms of a very inefficient transport system.

Table 4.3 provides data on the different modes plying in Dhaka. According to the DITS, the total number of buses required for a reasonable level of public transport in the city in 1993/94 was 4,000. If we assume an annual population growth rate of 7%, more than 5000 are needed today. As shown in the table, this number is nominally met, but far fewer than 5,000 operate on any given day. More than two thirds of these are dilapidated and more than 10 years old. Only about 200 are of "standard" quality. Due to a lack of available financing, the fleets are not being expanded.

Table 4.3 Dhaka Vehicle Estimates, 1997

	Number of Vehicles	Average Annual utilisation (km)	Total annual vehicle travel (million km)	Fuel economy (km/l)
Cars & taxis	42,000	19,200	806	8.0
Jeep, station wagon, microbus	12,000	19,200	230	8.0
Minibus	4,000	57,600	230	4.8
Diesel bus	5,000	64,000	320	2.4
Diesel truck	14,500	38,400	557	2.4
Motorised 3-wheeler	31,000	40,000	1,240	20.0
Motorised 2-wheeler	73,500	10,000	735	35.0
Cycle rickshaw	100,000	N/A	N/A	N/A

Source: Xie *et al*, 1999.

Another unfortunate characteristic of transport in Dhaka is that women have very poor access to bus facilities due to extreme overcrowding. Conditions are often intolerable or even unsafe for women due to competition for available passenger space on buses.

Air pollution caused by motor vehicles has reached critical proportions and has become a major health problem. Motor vehicles account for 30% to 50% of the hydrocarbon emissions, 40% to 60% of the NO_x and almost all of the CO emissions in urban centres. A recent study by the World Bank reveals a worsening trend. According to the report, exhaust from two-stroke engines used in auto-rickshaws and fumes from diesel buses and trucks contribute more than 60% of the total air pollution in Dhaka (although Table 4.4 shows that this figure varies considerably by pollutant). At the same time, noise pollution from poorly muffled two and three-wheelers has also become a major health hazard, especially for the drivers and passengers of those vehicles.

Table 4.4 Estimated Vehicle Emissions Factors
(grams/kilometre)

	Particulate matter (PM10)	Nitrogen oxides (NO$_x$)	Non-methane hydrocarbons (NMHC)	Carbon monoxide (CO)
Private car gasoline	0.2	1.6	3.6	24.9
Taxis	0.3	3.2	6.0	40.0
Minibus	0.9	2.5	0.5	1.3
Diesel bus	2.0	8.3	1.3	4.4
Diesel truck	2.0	6.5	1.3	3.4
Motorised 3-wheeler – gasoline	0.8	0.1	10.9	13.2
Motorised 3-wheeler – CNG	0.1	0.2	0.8	0.8
Motorised 2-wheeler	0.8	0.1	4.5	7.9

Source: Carter et al, 1998, except data for 3-wheelers, from Environment Canada testing.

Ambient air quality data from the Department of Environment (Table 4.5) show alarming levels of pollution around the city, especially suspended particulate matter (SPM) and sulphur dioxide (SO$_2$). Nitrogen oxide (NO$_x$) levels, though still within tolerable limits, are expected to rise with increasing traffic volumes. Damage to human health is also growing alarmingly, with consequent impacts on productivity and incomes. The World Bank recently (1999-2000) estimated the health costs to the city population from particulate (PM$_{10}$) pollution from diesel buses and trucks at over TK 590 million annually (about $10 million). The total cost of air pollution in Dhaka City was estimated to be as high as $250 million per year including very high costs related to lead exposure – although lead exposure is presumably declining since lead was phased out of gasoline in 1999.

Current Bus System

The bus system in Dhaka is characterised by a large number of individual bus owners, about 750, with an average of only 2 buses per owner. Following are general observations about present day bus services:

Table 4.5 Air Quality in Different Areas of Dhaka, 1996-97
(micrograms per cubic meter)

Parameter	Farmgate	Gulshan	Tejgaon	Gabtali	Mohakali	Indust.	Comm.	Resid.
						Proposed standards		
SPM						500	400	200
(night)	424	402	424	590	450			
(day)	2235	502	686	998	950			
NO$_2$						100	100	80
(night)	15	3	3	15	3			
(day)	46	48	46	54	48			
SO$_2$						120	100	80
(night)	56	64	39	110	94			
(day)	163	200	129	181	150			

Note: Areas are five neighbourhoods around the city, with Gulshan the furthest from the urban core.

- The quality of buses is very low. Many do not have window panes. Most are more than ten years old. Many were purchased as used trucks and later converted to buses. They are mostly diesel and emit high levels of particulates and black smoke. New buses cost between $25,000 and $50,000. Most of these are imported from India or are built in Dhaka by fitting new bus bodies onto truck chassis.

- Existing bus routes are not based on any origin-destination surveys. There are no specifications for required level of service on the routes, nor enforcement that buses run on specified routes.

- Schedules exist for some routes but are not maintained. Buses compete with each other for passengers, often double or triple parking in order to pick up passengers at busy locations. This results in traffic delays, congestion and reckless driving. This particular form of competition has not proven to be beneficial to the travelling public as it offers neither regularity nor dependability of service.

- The highly fragmented nature of the bus industry, lack of resources for maintenance and lack of professional management result in under-utilisation of fleets and low productivity.

- Individual operators have little incentive or commitment to provide good service.

Dhaka's many vehicle types compound traffic and air quality problems (courtesy Roland Wong, BEMP).

There are two major companies, one state-owned (the Bangladesh Road Transport Corporation, BRTC) and the other private (the Metro Bus Company). Each provides about five percent of bus transport services. The Metro Bus Company, with about 100 buses, serves two commuter routes. While these companies could provide the seeds for better bus service in the future, they are probably too small to be efficient in service, or to have the ressources to purchase high-quality, low emission buses.

Recent Initiatives

Several major transport-related initiatives are under way in Dhaka:

Phase-out of Unleaded Gasoline. Bangladesh rapidly phased out leaded gasoline beginning in July, 1999. Since the country has only one refinery and imports about two-thirds of its gasoline as product, the process consisted mainly of a switch to importing high-octane unleaded fuel, and blending this with their domestically-produced gasoline.

Dhaka Urban Transport Project (DUTP). The DUTP has the dual goals of improving road transport infrastructure and strengthening the management and planning of the transport network. It is a multi-stakeholder project led by the Bangladesh government, with strong support from the World Bank. To date the project has produced a master plan for transport development and a plan for rationalising the bus route system in Dhaka.

According to Iqbal Karim, transport specialist with the World Bank, the project envisages good bus services provided by the private sector to be the main thrust of public transportation in Dhaka. To help make bus services more efficient, the project will provide for bus lanes, designated bus stops, and improvements of bus terminals and depots that are currently major sources of traffic congestion in the city. The project will also deregulate fares and encourage commercial credit for bus entrepreneurs to improve competition. Several of these measures are already underway[17].

Dhaka Air Quality Management Project (AQMP). This initiative focuses on air-quality monitoring and improvement, through actions such as implementing a vehicle inspection and maintenance programme. The World Bank has provided a $5 million loan for activities under this programme.

Vehicle conversion to CNG. Domestic natural gas is abundant and the government has set its price for transport at about half the price per kilometre of gasoline. The government also supports projects to convert vehicles to CNG. Several hundred government vehicles have been converted to date. A recent project led by private entrepreneurs and assisted by the Canadian International Development Agency (CIDA), the UN Development Program (UNDP) and the Danish Agency for Development Assistance (DANIDA) will help introduce CNG regulations and safety standards and train mechanics and engineers on conducting CNG vehicle conversions. It will also initiate a programme to convert three-wheel "autorickshaws" in Dhaka from gasoline to CNG, keeping the existing two-stroke engines. This effort may also be expanded to convert buses to CNG and acquire new CNG buses, discussed below.

Premium Bus Project. Since 1997, several private companies have been operating a "premium bus service" along two major commuter corridors in Dhaka. The service features air conditioned, coach-style buses, with seated riding only. Frequent departures during rush hour and pre-paid ticketing help speed boarding and travel times. Ticket prices are deregulated and are currently being set by operators at about double the price of standard buses. The service has proven popular with relatively wealthy residents, and one survey indicates that a substantial share of riders own cars but prefer to take the premium buses, as driving in Dhaka is difficult and tiring.

---

17   Personal Communication, Iqbal Karim, World Bank, Dhaka.

National Land Transport Policy. With the assistance of the Department for International Development (DFID), the Ministry of Communications is drafting a National Land Transport Policy to create more efficient transport systems, a better environment and safer travel conditions. The policy includes the development of bus transport, including government support for improved infrastructure, better regulatory practice and a comprehensive bus plan for Dhaka.

Pilot Bus Project

In order to augment the role of the private sector in urban transport, the government has taken as a first step the partial deregulation of transit tariffs, to encourage the expansion of transit services. It has implemented a two-tier tariff system, with unregulated fares for higher quality services and continued control of fares for ordinary services to ensure affordability for the poor.

Developing a fully market-based bus system will be difficult. Any major overhaul of the system will create winners and losers and engender strong opposition. It also risks being poorly designed. Therefore, a pilot or demonstration project for buses has been generally endorsed. Initial plans call for:

- Selection of a particular route from among identified candidates.

- Selection of buses for the route based on optimum capacity and fleet size.

- Professional management and economic viability of bus operations.

- Use of a bus depot that is equipped with proper maintenance facilities;

- Measures and monitoring to minimise environmental impacts.

- Creation of a favourable investment environment. Five-year vehicle loans are currently in the 14% range.

- Infrastructure upgrades to allow fast bus travel. Average transit bus speeds in Dhaka are currently below 10 km/hr.

- Other infrastructure upgrades such as better pedestrian facilities and bus stops.

- Raising public awareness of the new bus route and its benefits.

As part of the Dhaka Urban Transport Project, 37 potential pilot routes were identified that have acceptable corridor dimensions and sufficient travel to support high speed, high capacity buses. Dhaka city is expanding in a north-south direction, and consequently, the growth in passenger demand is highest along north-south corridors. Consequently, a north-south corridor appears to be the logical choice for the first demonstration bus route and one of these has been selected.

Demand is heavy along this corridor and there are encouraging actions by the government to ensure better traffic flows and enforcement of traffic rules. Taking into consideration a bus capacity of 50 passengers, occupancy of 60%, fleet utilisation rate of 80% and headway of 2 minutes, the number of buses required for this route has been estimated to be about 95. Initial plans are to put 20-25 new, clean-fuel buses into service on this route under the licensing and operating rules established by the pilot project. The fleet size can later be increased as revenues permit and demand requires.

Use of CNG buses. Given the state of air pollution in an around the city, the pilot project also targets demonstration of buses that use an environment-friendly fuel. Given the unavailability of clean-diesel fuel in Dhaka, and the good availability of natural gas, combined with the success in developing CNG conversion programmes for government vehicles and three-wheel autorickshaws, CNG appears an obvious choice for buses.

CNG can also displace some petroleum imports and relieve the pressure on Bangladesh's scarce foreign currency. Bangladesh's crude oil imports have been increasing by about 10% per year (except 1995-96) and refined products have increased at twice that rate, contributing toward balance-of-payments problems for the country. A final reason to test CNG buses is it will fit in with a bigger programme to develop a gas distribution infrastructure in Dhaka. Additional refuelling stations for the bus demonstration project will also be able to supply the growing number of other CNG vehicles on the roads.

Ownership and financing. A private company, supported by the government, will purchase, own and operate the bus fleet for Dhaka's pilot project. Though public-private partnerships have worked successfully in other countries, Dhaka lacks private investors. Therefore, initial financing likely will be sought from external sources, such as international agencies.

Professional management. Two companies using professional managers will operate the fleet. One company will be responsible for bus financing, maintenance, parking, training of drivers and mechanics, and provision of CNG. The other company will be a co-operative of various owners responsible for bus operation, routing and scheduling. Bus manufacturers will be expected to provide mechanics for the first year of operation and help train local mechanics. Innovative fare collection methods will be implemented.

Economic viability. The existing premium bus service charges Taka 1.0 (about two US cents) for every passenger kilometre. Standard bus fare is Tk 0.6. Because of the low price of CNG, it is estimated that air-conditioned CNG bus service can be provided at a price below Tk 1.0. Table 4.6 provides a breakdown of estimated operating costs for the CNG buses.

How the Pilot Project Could be Strengthened

A major problem with this project is that it is likely to be implemented in a somewhat piecemeal manner. For example, financing for the buses may proceed before the infrastructural improvements along the route are fully developed. Among other things, this could preclude selection of bus specifications that are integrated with planned bus stop features. Developing a more detailed, integrated plan before commencing implementation appears important.

External assistance in the following areas could be helpful:

- Involving technical experts to help fully develop elements of the pilot project and ensure that the final implementation plan is "best practice". Involving cities that have already implemented BRT systems can also help reduce the time and cost of developing a detailed implementation plan in Dhaka.

- Understanding how other cities (like Bogota) have involved stakeholder groups such as bus manufacturers and local operators to reflect their concerns and gain their support.

- Raising the visibility (and glamour) of the project to increase political support and provide momentum toward making it a reality.

A key, and potentially difficult, part of the project will be working with the Bangladesh and Dhaka governments to develop new regulations for the demonstration route and gain approval for physical improvements in the corridor. Though the recently elected national government in Dhaka has

Table 4.6 Estimates of CNG Bus Operating Costs
(Taka)

Cost Item	CNG bus (air-conditioned)	CNG bus (Non-air- conditioned)
Fixed Cost (Taka per year)		
Crew wages	162,000	162,000
Overhead and other fixed costs	50,000	50,000
Insurance	36,000	36,000
Fees and taxes	5,450	5,450
Vehicle (amortisation)[a]	558,748	446,748
Subtotal	812,198	700,198
Annual fixed cost		
Daily fixed cost for vehicle @ 300 working days per year	2,538	2,188
Hourly fixed cost for vehicle @ 300 working days per year	159	137
Fixed cost per vehicle-km	12.7	10.9
Fixed cost per passenger-km	0.32	0.38
Variable cost (taka per vehicle or unit km)[b]		
Fuel	3.15	3.15
Lubricants	0.40	0.40
Tyres & tubes	1.48	1.48
Batteries	0.25	0.25
Repair and maintenance	1.71	1.71
Variable cost / vehicle-km	6.99	6.99
Variable cost /passenger-km[c]	0.14	0.14
Operating cost/vehicle km (fixed costs/ vehicle km and variable costs/passenger km)	19.68	17.93
Bottom line: operating cost/passenger-km	Tk 0.68	Tk 0.62

Source: Sabu Hossain, 2002, personal communication.

Note: As of June 2002, Tk52 = $1.

a. CNG bus cost calculated based on price of Tk 2,400,000 (air conditioned), 2,000,000 (non-air-conditioned). Amortisation on 80% of purchase price. Residual value of Tk 0 after 5 years, interest rate of 14%. As of January 2002.

b. Based on an average of 60,000 km per year.

c. Based on bus capacity of 48 passengers and average occupancy of 29 passengers (60%).

indicated strong support for the project, several stakeholder groups could try to delay it. Nevertheless, the general sense of urgency to do something about Dhaka's traffic problems provides an incentive for all to push this project forward as fast as possible.

Another area of concern is in the fragmented nature of the bus industry in Dhaka. While a tender may not be used for the pilot project, competitive tenders will best serve future expansions. Whether there are enough groups to compete effectively for such tenders is unclear. To avoid one company gaining a strong advantage over other companies, it may be necessary to encourage groups of smaller bus companies to form co-operatives in order to compete effectively.

The Dhaka pilot bus project is a promising opportunity to promote sustainable transport in one of the world's poorest cities, before the entire road system is ceded to motorcycles and cars serving a tiny fraction of the population. Dhaka desperately needs a boost to its transit system and a demonstration that buses can provide quality travel service.

SAO PAULO, BRAZIL

Sao Paulo, which dominates the vast hinterland of one of Brazil's wealthiest agricultural states, is the country's commercial, financial, and industrial centre. As the capital and largest city of Brazil and of South America, it is an ultramodern metropolis with skyscrapers, palatial homes, and spacious parks and recreational facilities. The city is also a major hub for Brazil's road, rail and air transport networks, and features a modern metro system. Its rapid economic development and population growth since the 1960s, however, have been accompanied by serious air and water pollution and overcrowding.

Seven years ago, for example, the 20-kilometre commute by car from the southern suburbs into Sao Paulo took about 45 minutes. This soon grew to one hour; and now daily traffic jams can extend for 240 kilometre while commuters sit bumper-to-bumper in very poor air for an hour and a half. Despite its potential to alleviate both congestion and air pollution, the public transportation system continues to lose patronage. Almost anyone who can, uses a private car rather than the "unfriendly" bus transit system, where passengers receive minimum services and find themselves standing in a crowd of 11 people per square metre.

With the proliferation of private vehicles, average vehicle speeds have slowed from an average of 30 km/hr down to 20, and heading toward 15. In short, Sao Paulo is under increasing pressure to implement transportation and emissions-control programmes so as to avoid "Bangkok-style" gridlock and "Mexico City-style" air-quality problems.

Current Transport System and Recent Initiatives

The Sao Paulo Metropolitan Region (SPMR) covers 8000 square kilometres and has 16 million inhabitants spread unevenly across 39 municipalities. The SPMR generates roughly 20% of GNP and is the most important economic region of the country. Each day, 30 million trips take place in the SPMR. Ten million of these are on foot. Forty-one percent of the motorised trips are by private automobile, 39% are by bus (mostly private operators), 14% by metro and six percent by train. Of the 12 million trips by public transit, about one-third involve a modal transfer. Specifically, 78% of metro trips, 61% of train trips and 16% of bus trips involve one or more modal transfers. Urban transport dominated by road-based motorised modes has significant impacts on the SPMR's environment. Despite a 250 kilometre rail network, the lack of integration between the metro and the suburban trains discourages rail trips in favour of buses and cars, creating heavy congestion during peak hours.

Public transportation in Sao Paulo relies heavily on the bus system. Since 1977, the fleet and the service provided by buses have stagnated. While the population of Sao Paulo grew by more than 6.5 million during this period, and the number of private automobiles increased three-fold (to 3.1m), the bus population in Sao Paulo grew only 25%, and the share of public-transport trips fell from 61% to 51%. With approximately 20,000 buses in the SPMR, competition for urban road space between buses and other traffic is a daily struggle. While public buses are theoretically given preference through measures such as parking restrictions along bus routes, this does little to enhance bus flows or make buses a more attractive option. As a result, buses are subject to the general traffic conditions prevailing throughout the area. Brazil's most important economic centre loses an estimated $300 million a year to traffic congestion and an incalculable amount to poor air quality; local and national planners are beginning to take notice.

Emissions data from Brazil are limited. Nonetheless, available data point to high levels of several important pollutants. The predominance of vehicle emissions come from cars, not buses. Ten years ago, 50% of city smog resulted from factories and 50% from motor vehicles. Today, the shares are 10% and 90% respectively. Excessive levels of carbon monoxide, ozone, and particulates have degraded air quality to the extent that Sao Paulo is among the world's ten worst cities, with its air pollution linked to elevated mortality rates and high incidences of respiratory and cardiovascular diseases.

Table 4.7 shows that Sao Paulo air quality is much worse than the neighbouring, less-industrial city of Rio de Janeiro, and also worse than US cities typically regarded as having serious transportation-related air quality problems.

Table 4.7 Comparison of Emissions with Other Cities
(1000 tonnes/year, 1997)

	HC	CO	NO_x	SO_x	PM
Sao Paulo	405.3	1,703.6	353.4	35.0	28.4
Rio de Janeiro	108.6	637.7	53.3	10.2	6.4
Chicago	214.7	N/A	245.3	13.4	N/A
Los Angeles	318.1	N/A	399.6	39.4	N/A

Source: USEPA, 1999. N/A = not available.

The federal government has established emissions standards for all new vehicles, as well as heavy-duty vehicle inspection programmes. As a result, today new vehicles in Brazil typically have fuel injection, catalytic converters, and fuel vapour adsorbers (canisters). A system of emissions laboratories and testing stations has also been put in place.

The government, together with Petrobras and Anfaeva (the national union of car manufacturers), has also pursued improvements in fuel quality. Lead has been removed from gasoline, alcohol is mixed with gasoline and tar and sulphur levels in diesel have been reduced. The improvements in emissions through time are shown in Table 4.8. Emissions of CO, HC, NO_x, and CHO (acetaldehyde, a toxic) for light vehicles have been reduced by up to 98%.

Table 4.8 Sao Paulo Emissions Comparisons by Fuel for Light-duty Vehicles (grams/km)

	Fuel	CO	HC	NOx	CHO
1980-83	Gasool	33.0	3.0	1.4	0.05
	Alcool	18.0	1.6	1.0	0.16
1990	Gasool	13.3	1.4	1.4	0.04
	Alcool	10.8	1.3	1.2	0.11
1995	Gasool	4.7	0.6	0.6	0.03
	Alcool	4.6	0.7	0.7	0.04
1999	Gasool	0.7	0.1	0.2	0.01
	Alcool	0.6	0.2	0.2	0.01

Source: IBAMA, 2000.

Note: "Gasool" is approximately 75% gasoline, 25% ethanol; "Alcool" is pure alcohol. CHO is acetaldehyde, a toxic.

Although Inspection and maintenance programmes exist, they appear to focus more on brakes and tail lights than on tailpipe emissions. Fines are issued for failing emissions inspections; visible polluters can be cited on the street. Enforcement appears lax, however, and even state-owned buses emit visible black smoke.

In February 2000, the Secretary of State for Metropolitan Transport (STM) introduced the Integrated Urban Transport Plan (PITU) for 2020 (STM, 2000). It estimates that unless actions are taken, the transport system will reach chaos by 2020:

■ Private car trips will grow by 69% over 1997 levels.

■ The public transport share of motorised trips will decline from 51% in 1997 to 45% in 2020.

■ The time spent on private car trips will grow approximately 20% over 1997 levels.

■ Traffic speed in the extended downtown area will decrease another 15% during peak hours.

■ The concentration of carbon monoxide in the extended downtown area will increase 32%.

- Easy accessibility to goods and services for the low-income population will decrease 21% in comparison to 1997.

- The cost of private car trips will increase 51% due to slower traffic speeds.

As shown in Table 4.9, from 1987 to 1997 growth in public transportation trips remained almost flat, while automobile trips nearly doubled. Public transport share in the modal split fell from 61% to 51%, while the motorization rate (number of cars per 1,000 inhabitants) rose sharply.

Table 4.9 Sao Paulo Transport Indicators

	Units	1977	1987	1997
Population	(x 1000)	10,273	14,248	16,792
Daily motorised trips	(x 1000)	15,758	18,750	20,620
Daily public transport trips	(x 1000)	9,759	10,455	10,472
Daily automobile trips	(x 1000)	6,240	8,295	10,148
% of trips on public transport	(%)	61.9%	55.8%	50.8%
Number of automobiles	(x 1000)	1,384	2,014	3,095
Motorization rate	(Cars per 1000 population)	135	141	184

Source: PITU 2020 (STM, 2000).

The PITU 2020 initiative includes both an urban planning and transport planning approach that sets objectives and attempts to garner regional political support for action. It is unclear to what extent the very difficult political and investment decisions outlined in this plan will be addressed, but Sao Paulo planners are hoping that the plan will lead to solutions – and not just marginal improvements. By putting transport issues on the public agenda, it is hoped the PITU will generate the public support needed for large-scale change. There are hopeful signs: the PITU process has already led to much improved co-ordination among all of the surrounding municipalities.

The PITU 2020 also includes an aggressive investment policy to develop new metropolitan bus and rail transit lines, terminals and stations, and to better regulate traffic. Specific objectives and actions contained in the PITU are summarised in Table 4.10.

Table 4.10 Summary of PITU 2020 Objectives
(R$ million)

Area of focus		Actions	Features	Cost
Rail services	Subway network	Construction of new subway lines	284 km of subway lines	21,820
	Special train from airport	Connect Congonhas, Guarulhos and Campo de Marte airports	44 km of special train lines	880
	Approach train	Upgrade lines; improve rolling stock, catenary and signalling system	88 km of improvements	440
	Regional train	Connect city to Campinas, Sorocaba and Sao Jose urban centres	177 km of restored train lines	874
Tire-based services	Metro bus	Implementation of bus corridors and junctions – EMTU	300 km of exclusive corridors	223
	Municipal bus system	Construct light vehicle and segregated corridors	260 km of segregated corridors	1,596
	Complementary system	Implement microbus circular line in the expanded downtown area	200 kilometre, single lane	33
Road infra-structure	Metro road planning	Build new connections, higher capacity, improved intersections	262 km of improvements	226
	Highway concessions	Improve highways	123 km of improvements	519
	Rodoanel road	Conclude works	121 km of improvements	2,562
	Planning for traffic and road net	Continue works	149 km of improvements	283
	Expansion of road network capacity	Construct priority traffic rings at main intersections	52 intersections; 15 km of network improvements	527
Traffic management	Urban toll	Implement downtown tolls of R$1.00	233 km of toll roads	15
	Central parking lots	Construct underground garages	30 lots, 11,400 vehicles	223
	Peripheral parking lots	Build parking lots near rail stations	40 lots, 26,300 vehicles	91
Total				30,312

Source: PITU 2020 (STM, 2000).

Through these types of initiatives, the PITU 2020 aims for:

- A two million hour per year reduction in time lost by public transport users during peak hours through service improvements – worth about $1 Billion per year.

- Improvement in the comfort and safety of public transportation.

- A 40% reduction in bus pollutant emissions.

- Substantial noise reductions.

- An 8% reduction in fuel consumption.

- A 35% reduction in traffic accidents.

- Greater downtown accessibility and development of new residential and commercial areas, with less traffic in the city centre.

- Better land use through urban renovation and development of "brownfield" and under-utilised areas.

Bus System Initiatives

There are two types of buses in Sao Paulo, large publicly regulated, privately owned buses and small privately owned and largely unregulated buses and vans. Recent initiatives affect both types:

Public buses/Private concessions. Buses are privately owned and operated under concessions from the municipal government. Within the city Sao Paulo Transporte S/A (SPTrans) manages 11,000 buses operated by 60 companies. SPTrans issues operational concessions, manages routes and collects fares. On the periphery of Sao Paulo, Empresa Metropolitana de Transportes Urbanos de Sao Paulo (EMTU/SP) operates on a similar scale.

Bus companies turn their collected fares over to a central collection agency. These revenues are then redistributed to the companies based on passenger kilometres and other factors. Further changes, including privatisation, are planned in order to improve service and reduce emissions. Price of concessions will be linked to pollution reductions. Investments in new and cleaner bus technology will qualify bus companies to receive additional compensation per kilometre over what the standard formula provides. The goal is to provide companies with an incentive for better maintenance, better engines and improved routing.

Small buses. The previous government opened the market to small buses and vans, in part to try to alleviate high unemployment rates. Small buses are unregulated and don't pay taxes; as they increase their ride share at the expense of larger buses, the revenue pool available for large buses declines. This puts additional pressure on transit bus companies to think twice about new investments. A new plan, nicknamed ORCA, attempts to deal with this problem by qualifying small buses and formalising the system, including regulating routes and fares. Many bus companies, however, have avoided participating in this system. Still, public acceptance of the programme is quite good and service has improved, including free transfers, better route information for passengers, and improved driver behaviour.

Despite the recent programmes, bus service in Sao Paulo continues to be fairly poor. Average bus speeds are low, around 13-to-14 km/hr, headways vary greatly, and service reliability is poor. For users of public transport, this situation has been chaotic. Many buses are old and uncomfortable, and often full. The low-income population living in the outskirts of the city spends up to four hours commuting by public transit each day. Bus operations are hindered by a number of factors. These include the on-board ticket collection system and poor accessibility for bus passengers at bus stops, which creates longer boarding and alighting times. The current traffic signal timing logic tends to favour the flow of automobiles.

However, in contrast to several other case study cities in this project, Sao Paulo has made considerable progress in developing "Bus Rapid Transit" systems. The city has undertaken a variety of initiatives to improve bus operations.

Bus lanes. Reserved or exclusive bus lanes have been incorporated in about 100 kilometres of arterial streets. These lanes are roughly divided between curb-side lanes (52 km) and median lanes (46 km). In most cases, bus lanes are separated from general traffic lanes by rubber stud dividers. These types of bus lanes can be constructed rapidly at low cost and are easy to abolish if problems arise. They are, therefore, quite attractive to traffic authorities. Yet they also pose several problems, such as conflicts with turning vehicles and (especially for curb-side lanes) with freight loading/unloading operations. Furthermore, in the absence of constant enforcement, regular traffic tends to invade the reserved lanes and mix with bus flows. They therefore require a high degree of supervision and enforcement. This problem is much less serious in cities such as Bogota and Curitiba that use larger barriers between bus lanes and other lanes.

BRT lines. Besides reserved bus lanes, the city has developed four "trunk-line" bus corridors with a total length of 62 kilometres (Table 4.11). These corridors include:

- Systematic control of bus operations, which leads to higher bus speeds and better service. The bus fleet may even be reduced because of quicker turnaround times.

- The concentration of passenger trips with common end points along a corridor warrants trunk-line infrastructure and high capacity buses. The numerous origins and destinations beyond the corridor ends require that integration terminals be provided to concentrate and distribute those trips across the corridor's area of influence.

Table 4.11 Trunkline Bus Corridors in the Sao Paulo Metropolitan Region

Corridor	Length (km)	Integration terminals	Bus fleet[a]	Volume of buses (peak-hour)[b]	Passengers per day (000)
Municipal					
Paes de Barros	3.4	1	61	57	64
Nove de Julho	14.6	2	1,392	270	304
Vila Nova Cachoerinha	11.0	1	226	177	199
Metropolitan					
Sao Mateus-Jabaquara	32.6	9	367	265	192

a. On trunk and other lines.
b. In the most travelled section of the corridor.
Source: World Bank, 1995.

The Sao Paulo Municipality Busway Privatisation Program. This was an attempt to optimise Sao Paulo's bus system by giving buses priority in traffic circulation and improving the existing road network. This programme also included a plan to reduce the level of subsidies paid by the existing public transport company (ex-CMTC, now Sao Paulo Transporte S.A.) due to inefficient operation, by transferring the operation to private companies. Finally, it sought to improve bus services by accelerating infrastructure investments postponed by previous administrations.

The planned programme included the introduction of a trunk-line bus corridor system fed by other lower volume corridors, use of high-capacity buses, and greater integration with other bus systems and other modes, such as the metro and suburban trains. In addition, users would pay a single tariff per trip without extra payments. Unfortunately, this imaginative programme failed to materialise because of financing problems. The revenue sharing plan, involving paying bus operators per kilometre, did not have acceptable safeguards to guarantee the needed loans.

Under PITU 2020, early steps toward improvement will be to re-evaluate the routes and route service – through a bidding plan in three areas. There are several plans for potential new rapid bus corridors and creative ways will be sought to identify more direct routes, possibly using the natural valley geography of Sao Paulo. High-speed busways are expected to increase average bus speeds to 24 km/hr, from the current average of 14 km/hr.

Promoting Cleaner Buses

Unlike many developing countries, Brazil has a large, modern, well-equipped and competitive bus-manufacturing industry, that builds up to 20,000 units a year – equal to Western Europe. Mercedes-Benz, Volkswagen, Scania and Volvo each have state-of-the-art truck and bus chassis plants in Brazil. They are matched by large body-manufacturing companies, notably Marco Polo and Busscar. Brazil exports significant numbers of buses to the rest of Latin America.

Although automobiles cause most vehicle emissions, STM has recognised the need to reduce emissions from 20,000 ageing diesel buses in order to achieve PITU air quality objective. The targeted 40% reduction in bus emissions cannot be achieved through inspection and maintenance alone and will necessarily involve difficult technology and fuel choices.

Although heavy-duty diesel engines have proven reliable and efficient for urban buses, both SPTrans and EMTU, the public bus companies, operate poorly maintained, ageing bus fleets using low grade, high sulphur content diesel fuel. Diesel engines in trucks and buses contribute over 50% of air-borne particulate matter in the bus corridors and up to six percent of total nitrogen oxides in Sao Paulo.

The sulphur content of Brazilian diesel fuel reaches up to 0.1% (1,000 ppm). According to SPTrans, the city's diesel fuel is at best 500 ppm. Although the national oil company Petrobras has stated that it is willing to upgrade its diesel production lines to European standards, this would require an estimated investment of R$ 3.5 billion (about $1.2 billion). There are few economic or political incentives to invest in such improvements.

According to bus manufacturers like Scania, Euro-III-certified engines will be available in Brazil at the end of 2002. Globalisation of bus markets is, in part at least, motivating introduction of Euro-III engines three to four years earlier than the standards require. This means that new buses will be cleaner than required, although they may not be able to achieve Euro-III emissions levels running on high-sulphur diesel fuel.

CNG programmes. About ten years ago, the Federal government of Brazil decided to reduce bus emissions by requiring all new buses to use CNG. Private bus companies were required to convert their fleet to CNG at the rate of 10% per year to reach 100% by 2001. The number of CNG buses reached 400, but various obstacles inhibited the programme and only 225 CNG buses remain in service. The CNG programme failed in Sao Paulo for reasons similar to those experienced in Europe and North America. Problems included:

- The city found it difficult to build pipeline extensions to the 68 bus garages scattered throughout Sao Paulo. Without an adequate fuel supply, operators had little incentive to purchase CNG buses.

- CNG buses are more expensive than diesel buses. A taxi can be converted for $1,000 to $2,000 with a payback from fuel savings in about 5 months. The conversion cost for buses is much higher at around $20,000, yielding a payback period of at least five years.

- Most of the private bus companies are financially unstable, and the revenue payback system discourages major investments. The city is in debt to the bus companies, which are often not fully compensated for their cost of delivering service. No new buses of any kind were purchased during the last 3 years.

- Although natural gas costs less than half the cost of gasoline ($0.35/l v. $0.70/l), it is a regulated fuel and the profit margins on resale for transportation use are considerably lower than for residential use.

- Considerable bus company revenues come from resale of their buses to other localities. Second-hand buses fetch low prices, and most rural localities have no capacity for dealing with advanced, alternative-fuel technologies like CNG. Sao Paulo bus operators have little incentive to purchase CNG buses, which have no established resale market.

Ethanol programmes. Prompted by the increase in oil prices in the 1970s, Brazil began to produce ethanol from sugar cane for use in automobiles. The programme was successful and pure ethanol (*alcool*) is used in approximately 40% of the cars. The remaining vehicles use *gasool*, a blend that ranges in composition but is typically around 25% ethanol and 75% gasoline. A weak distribution system and strikes by sugar cane workers, however, sent ethanol prices soaring in the late 1980s. When oil prices dropped at about the same time, the programme lost momentum. Today fewer than one percent of new cars sold in Brazil run on pure ethanol.

Despite the domestic availability of ethanol and a desire to improve Sao Paulo's air quality and fuel-distribution infrastructure, the use of ethanol in buses has never gone beyond the experimental stage. Although Brazil is the world's single largest bus market and Swedish heavy truck and bus-maker Scania is the world's largest supplier of ethanol-powered buses, the market for ethanol buses has not materialised. Scania contends that operating costs are too high – with 70% higher fuel costs and lower energy content – for ethanol buses to be competitive. The company recently reconverted two ethanol buses to diesel and shipped two others back to Sweden because they could not sell them in Brazil.

Fuel cell programmes. The UN Development Program (UNDP) and the Global Environmental Facility (GEF) have initiated a project with the Brazilian Ministry of Mines and Energy's EMTU/SP (Empresa Metropolitana de Transportes Urbanos de Sao Paulo S/A) to stimulate the development and use of fuel-cell buses by testing them in the greater Sao Paulo Metropolitan Area. This project will provide initial experience in using fuel-cell buses, and achieve cost reductions, paving the way for further projects that will likely be necessary for fuel-cell buses to achieve commercial status.

Pending Brazilian government approval on financing arrangements, the project will move into Phase II, which involves running a fleet of three buses from one bus garage in the SPMR for four years in order to obtain experience. In Phase III a bus garage will be converted to handle a fleet of 200 fuel-cell buses. Buses supplied for Phase III are expected to be built in Brazil by adaptation of a Brazilian trolley-bus chassis, to take advantage of existing national capabilities. In Phase IV, buses will be produced commercially for wider use in the SPMR and other cities in Brazil. It is hoped that by this stage, fuel-cell buses will be economically competitive with diesel buses on a life-cycle basis.

STM is aware that fuel-cell buses will not be commercially viable at first. The motivations for participating in this early stage of development include:

■ Increasing awareness of fuel-cell technology and its benefits, and demonstrating to the public that STM considers air pollution to be a serious problem.

■ The desire to play a role in advancing the technology while sharing in the benefits.

■ The desire to begin building capacity to work with hydrogen. For this reason, the programme will remain in EMTU/public sector hands for training and learning. Universities will also be involved.

■ As Brazil is the largest bus manufacturer worldwide, it would like to create a foothold in the future fuel-cell bus market.

■ Since hydrogen can be produced from alcohol, Brazil would like to investigate development of the ethanol-hydrogen cycle for on-board processing.

Hybrid-electric buses. Diesel hybrid-electric buses are slated to run on the soon-to-be-completed southern loop busway, which connects to the metro. STM believes hybrids are already commercially viable. Also, because both hybrids and fuel cells use the same electric-drive system, hybrids provide useful experience in working with electric systems.

Bus Fleet Turnover: a Potential Approach to Cleaner Buses

Under the concession formula established in 1992, 80% of the city's payment to bus operators is based on the total bus kilometres travelled, and 20% is based on the number of passengers transported. This formula eliminates the direct relationship between fares collected and revenues earned, and encourages operators to provide services to the less populated and longer distance routes.

Over the last three years, reformulation of this system of concessions and reimbursement has been discussed. During this period, temporary one-year extensions of the existing system have been granted. However, uncertainty about new concession formulas and how new payback systems might work has reduced the incentive to make new capital investments: no new buses have been purchased since 1998. For SPTrans, this means that the average bus is now eight years old, v. three years old in 1992. Recent thinking is that concessions will cover a five-to-six year period and include stronger regulations that require advanced technologies – like those meeting Euro III or IV emissions standards.

Such a new system could trigger considerable interest in the acquisition of new buses, and spur rapid bus fleet turnover. In 1992, the introduction of new concessions led to the acquisition of 1,200 buses. With phased acquisitions required under new concessions, SPTrans expects to see up to 2,000 buses replaced per year over the life of the 6-year concessions, resulting in 11,000 new buses on the streets of Sao Paulo. With this level of bus acquisition and turnover, the opportunity exists for Sao Paulo to deploy large numbers of clean and advanced technology buses over the coming decade.

Assessment

Unfortunately, many of Sao Paulo's initiatives toward sustainable transportation have been difficult to introduce and enforce. This does not bode well for meeting a target of Euro-II compliance for all buses within five years. This will depend on the rate of new bus purchases, which will depend on incentives for investment, which in turn will depend upon the new concession agreements. The presence of good enforcement, supporting policies and allocations of tax expenditures will be important factors as well.

The expansion of rail transit and the construction of dedicated busways, as envisaged by STM's PITU 2020, will also be challenging. Although the failed Municipality Busway Privatisation Program was a good effort to integrate corridors and terminals and optimise the bus system, it demonstrated the difficulty of getting major capital projects off the ground.

However, Sao Paulo is an experienced and proud city, with a number of reasons for optimism about accomplishing the challenging objectives of the PITU 2020. These include:

- Growing political and social concern over mobility and air quality.

- Past efforts that demonstrate awareness and intent — and provide valuable lessons for the future. Sao Paulo is not starting from scratch. Previous investments and construction of metro lines and busways give STM a substantial foundation upon which to build.

- Regulators do not avoid challenges and have already introduced a number of important national regulations and standards.

- The SPMR generates roughly 20% of Brazil's GNP. As such, there exists substantial capital which could be tapped for investment in transit — if the political will is there.

- The demand for public transportation is a growth market and will expand tremendously over the next 20 years, especially if high quality services are provided. There are currently 60 million public transit trips per day in Brazil, with a potential for 80 million.

- Large bus fleet turnover is expected.

BANGALORE, INDIA

Bangalore, located in south central India, is the capital of the state of Karnataka. It is the fifth largest city in India with a population of about 6 million. It sits at an altitude of about 1,000 metres and has a relatively temperate climate despite its latitude (12 degrees north). It has been called the "Silicon Valley" of India due to its high concentration of computer and other high-tech firms. Bangalore is considered by many to be India's most liveable large city. Regional economic growth has been dramatic in recent years, as has population growth. Negative impacts of this growth include increasing traffic congestion and air pollution.

However, Bangalore's traffic is still much better than in other large Indian cities. Traffic appears to flow smoothly most of the time in most parts of the city. Motorists are disciplined; for example, they stop briskly when traffic signals turn red, and they generally avoid being caught in intersections during signal changes.

Many important institutions in local transport-related decision making are actually state institutions (e.g. the Karnataka Pollution Control Board and Karnataka Urban Infrastructure Development and Finance Corp). Several municipal agencies also play an important role, such as the Bangalore Metro Transit Corp. (BMTC), Bangalore City Corp. and Commissioner of Police.

The bus company, BMTC, is the focus of most transit-related issues. BMTC owns and operates the vast majority of transit buses in the city and metropolitan area, and may provide the best and most efficient bus service in India, with high average fuel efficiency and labour productivity. Frequent service is provided on most routes and buses are kept in relatively good condition.

BMTC is spearheading a new busway pilot project. Other agencies involved include those mentioned above, as well as the Bangalore Metro Regional Development Authority.

Current Transport Situation

Although Bangalore has much less traffic congestion than other large Indian cities, it nonetheless has significant congestion, which is likely to become much worse over the next few years, given the high growth rates in population and vehicle use. Particularly rapid growth in small vehicles, including cars as well as two- and three-wheelers, has reduced the space-efficiency of the roadway system. Buses represent a declining share of total vehicles and travel. As congestion increases, bus service deteriorates, which spurs greater use of personal vehicles. As in so many cities around the world, there is a need to revitalise public transport in order to break this vicious cycle.

Tables 4.12 and 4.13 below are based on data assembled for BMTC by Contrans (Contrans/CIRT 1999). The dominant motorised vehicle type in

Bangalore is the two-wheeler. Motorcycles and scooters are more numerous and account for more kilometres per year than all other modes combined. Buses, however, transport the largest number of people. BMTC buses account for half of all motorised passenger kilometres. "Maxicabs", typically 15-to-18 seat passenger vans, are a rapidly growing phenomenon – a paratransit service that is growing to fill a niche apparently underserved by existing public transit services. In order for BMTC to maintain its position and keep up with travel growth, many additional buses will be needed in coming years.

Table 4.12 Travel and Fuel-use Estimates for Bangalore, 2000

| | Number of vehicles (000) | Annual travel per vehicle (km) | Total vehicle travel (million km) | Average pass-engers per vehicle | Total passenger travel (million km) | Share of pass-enger travel | Fuel efficiency | | Annual fuel use (million litres) |
							km/litre	litre/ 100km	
Motorcycle	780	2,705	2,110	1.3	2,743	17.0%	25	4.0	84.4
Autorickshaw (3-wheeler)	85	2,153	183	1.8	329	2.0%	30	3.3	6.1
Car gasoline	145	3,628	526	2.5	1,315	8.1%	10	10.0	52.6
Car diesel	6	11,500	69	2.5	172	1.1%	14	7.1	4.9
Tractor	3	10,741	29	N/A	N/A	N/A	3	33.3	9.7
Bus BMTC	2	76,667	161	50	8,050	49.8%	4	25.0	40.3
Bus non-BMTC	9	76,667	690	N/A	N/A	N/A	4	25.0	172.5
Truck	33	9,970	329	N/A	N/A	N/A	3	33.3	109.7
Maxicab	4	55,116	237	15	3,555	22.0%	7	14.3	33.9

Source: Bangalore, 2000.

Bangalore's 1995 master development plan directs the manner in which the tremendous additional growth expected through 2010 is handled. A basic goal is to maintain fairly low population density within the city and direct much of the growth toward suburbs – in essence, planned sprawl. This represents an attempt to preserve the leafy calm atmosphere in the heart of the city. However, it may result in long travel distances and increased traffic congestion throughout the metropolitan area. More bus routes may be needed outside the central business district. On the other hand, density

Table 4.13 Vehicle Emissions Estimates for Bangalore, 2000

	CO			NO_x			PM		
	Average g/km	Total g/year	Pct of all transport	Average g/km	Total g/year	Pct of all transport	Average g/km	Total g/year	Pct of all transport
Motorcycle	10	21,100	62.0%	0.1	211	0.6%	5	10,550	27.5%
Autorickshaw	9	1,647	4.8%	0.15	27	0.1%	5	915	2.4%
Car gasoline (uncontrolled)	10	5,260	15.4%	6	3,156	8.9%	8	4,208	11.0%
Car gasoline (controlled)	0.2	N/A	N/A	2	N/A	N/A	0.5	N/A	N/A
Car diesel	1	69	0.2%	8	552	1.6%	5	345	0.9%
Tractor	2	58	0.2%	31	899	2.5%	18	522	1.4%
Bus BMTC	2	322	0.9%	24	3,864	10.9%	16	2,576	6.7%
Bus non-BMTC	2	1,380	4.1%	24	16,560	46.6%	16	11,040	28.8%
Truck	2	658	1.9%	24	7,896	22.2%	17	5,593	14.6%
Maxicab	15	3,555	10.4%	10	2,370	6.7%	11	2,607	6.8%

Source: Bangalore, 2000.

levels are high enough and there are enough bus riders throughout the region that there is no problem in keeping buses full. Bangalore does not appear likely to develop, anytime soon, the problem experienced by many North American cities of having such dispersed travel patterns that they prove difficult to serve with large buses on fixed routes.

Buses: Status and Future Planning

BMTC provides much, but not all, of the bus service in Bangalore. A number of private operators serve non-BMTC routes, particularly commuter routes. But BMTC is the main provider of regularly-scheduled bus service in downtown Bangalore. BMTC uses buses built by the two main Indian manufacturers – Ashok Leyland and Tata – with most buses of 80 passenger capacity. The age distribution is shown in Table 4.14.

BMTC buses are kept in fairly good condition. Tire treads are good, buses are frequently painted, and few produce visible smoke emissions. However, because one-third of the buses are over 10 years old and two-thirds are over five years old, with no tailpipe emission control, their emissions of NO_x and fine particulates are probably quite high.

Table 4.14 Age Distribution of Buses in Bangalore

Age bracket	Number of buses	Percent of total
< 1 year	135	7%
1-3 years	462	22%
3-5 years	174	8%
5-10 years	567	27%
> 10 years	752	36%
Total	2,090	100%

Source: Bangalore, 2000.

During 2001, BMTC created a new bus-system development plan, funded by SIDA, the Swedish International Development Agency. BMTC worked with the Swedish "Contrans" consulting group and the Indian research group "Central Institute of Road Transport". The report outlines a metro-area bus system for Bangalore through 2010, including a system of linked, dedicated bus routes loosely fashioned after Curitiba's system. The report includes a detailed phasing strategy for the plan. The first step is a pilot bus route to be developed during the first year and a half of the project, through 2003.

Pilot Bus Project

The pilot project focuses on a logical first step: developing a single roadway corridor within the city for dedicated bus services. The plan also calls for selection of a corridor that allows development of bus-only lanes while preserving one-to-two lanes in each direction for non-bus traffic, with some roadway widening where necessary. The plan also calls for use of modern, low-floor, large-capacity buses. The objective of the project is to demonstrate that through similar upgrades, the entire bus system could cost-effectively provide more rapid, comfortable service.

The pilot route selected by BMTC consists of a 12-kilometre corridor that runs through the heart of Bangalore, utilising relatively wide avenues for most of the distance. Initially 30 buses will operate on this route, with an average headway of three minutes or less. With 30 buses, three minute gaps between buses can be achieved with an average bus speed of about 15 km/hr. Obviously higher average speeds, which seem possible, would reduce these headway times.

The project also includes upgrading bus terminals at each end of the route and building new bus shelters along the route. During 2001 many new bus shelters were installed and one of the two terminals was completely rebuilt. The terminal includes extensive parking facilities for cars and two-wheelers, as well as space for a number of new retail stores. The redesigned terminal is an impressive structure and embraces the concept of "multi-modalism". Bus handling in the new terminal is also quite impressive, with a high "throughput" of buses.

How the Pilot Project Could be Strengthened

The project could be strengthened in at least two areas:

Traffic signalisation. An advanced system to control traffic signals at intersections, similar to what is being tested in Los Angeles, could be valuable. This could feature a low-cost system of transponders at each signal that detects the approach of buses, or something more ambitious, such as linking the signals into BRTC's existing GPS-based bus tracking system and allowing alignment of buses to maintain consistent headway times. Given the orderly traffic patterns in Bangalore, and the general respect for traffic signals, this project provides excellent opportunity to showcase such an advanced technology in the developing world.

Clean Fuels Testing. SIDA is considering a grant to provide Bangalore with new, modern buses on its pilot route. BRTC will continue to run older buses on other routes. This may create an opportunity to test out several clean fuel configurations on both types of bus, as well as advanced emission-control systems. Testing should include both emissions and durability. In a later phase it may be practical to consider testing more advanced bus technologies such as hybrids and fuel cells.

JAKARTA, INDONESIA

Situated in the north-west corner of the island of Java, Jakarta is a rapidly growing city of nearly 10 million people and an area of over 600 square kilometres. At six degrees south of the equator, it is hot and moist, as well as flat. The city's economy was growing at a rapid rate until 1997, when the Indonesian "economic/debt crisis" occurred. Growth rates throughout

Indonesia have been lower over the past five years and a series of debt crises and political problems have destabilised the country, causing increased unemployment and reduced foreign investment. Jakarta shows signs of being a "modern" city, including scattered high-rise office buildings, substantial highway infrastructure and a relatively large number of private cars and motorbikes (owned by about 10% of the population). Jakarta has more cars than Manila and more motorised vehicles than Singapore.

Recent decentralisation has given more power to the city government. This may make transportation improvements less dependant on National authorities than in some other capitals. However, the process is recent and on-going and it is unclear how true this will prove to be for any given project.

Current Transport System

Given the large geographic area of Jakarta, recent developments further out into the suburbs have created very long commutes for many residents. Between 1985 and 1993, the number of daily commuters from the suburbs to Jakarta increased four-fold. Rapid growth in highway infrastructure (six percent per year since between 1976 and 1994) has probably encouraged this suburbanization. But the highways are now heavily congested during the long rush-hour periods, thanks to an even more rapid nine percent annual growth-rate in vehicles (Sari and Susantono, 1999). A second roadway level has been added to some highways for high-occupancy vehicles and as a toll road.

These trends are expected to continue if strong measures are not taken to promote an alternative regional transport plan. However, since the increase in roadway capacity has been unable to keep up with the increase in car ownership, increases in congestion will probably slow travel growth unless massive road-building efforts are undertaken. But such expanding roads to allow more traffic would likely cause regional air quality to deteriorate to levels far worse than statutory limits. An alternative plan is needed to provide mobility to all while avoiding massive investments in roadway infrastructure and the resulting environmental impacts.

Jakarta features a variety of vehicle types, but one of the most common 10 years ago, the *becak*, is rarely seen today. These three-wheel, non-motorised taxis have traditionally provided inexpensive door-to-door service and feeder service to other forms of public transport. They have also provided a source of low-skill employment, particularly important for recent migrants from the surrounding countryside. Becaks were banned from most streets in Jakarta in 1990. They were replaced in large part by *bajaj*, three-wheel motorcycles, which are faster but noisy and highly polluting.

The current bus system in Jakarta uses what could be called "quantity licensing", basically route licenses granted by the government to different operators without co-ordinating service on each route. Licenses stipulate fleet size but do not regulate service quality aspects like bus frequency, reliability or safety. The average age of buses is about 7-10 years. Most are made by Toyota and are assembled in Jakarta.

Only a rudimentary set of data on vehicles, travel, and fuel use are available for Jakarta. These data are shown in Table 4.15.

Table 4.15 Vehicle and Travel Data for Jakarta, 1999

Vehicle type	Vehicle population	Average passenger capacity	Average annual utilisation (km)	Total annual travel (mil km)	Fuel economy (km/litre)
Cars/Light trucks*	1,218,632	5	N/A	N/A	8-10
Buses**	10,218	100 with standing	60,000	613	2 – 3.5
Angkots (vans used for paratransit)**	11,865	12-15	60,000	679	6-8
Motorised 2-wheelers*	1,543,603	2-3	N/A	N/A	40
Becaks (NMT 3 wheelers)***	0	2-3	N/A	N/A	N/A

Source: Pelangi, 2002.

Notes: N/A = not available.

*Study Integrated Transportation Master Plan for Jabotabek, 2001.

** Activities Monthly Report, February 2001, Department of Traffic DKI Jakarta.

*** Becaks have been banned in Jakarta since September 2001.

Jakarta suffers increasingly from emissions of particulates and other pollutants. The URBAIR report (1997) indicated that ambient concentrations of several pollutants routinely exceed statutory limits. Concentrations of sulphur dioxide and nitrogen oxides can be 50% above allowable limits, and particulate matter (PM) can be three times higher. Lead remains a problem, although leaded gasoline has started to be phased out. Recent inventory estimates indicate that vehicle emissions account for about half of airborne particulates, 75% of NO_x, and 90% of hydrocarbons.

Recent scenarios by Sari and Susantono (1999) estimated that if the economy rebounded to its earlier strength, the number of cars and amount of travel would increase about five-fold between 2000 and 2020. CO_2 emissions in Jakarta can be expected to grow at a similar rate.

Recent Initiatives

Several major transport-related initiatives are under way in Jakarta:

The Blue Skies Program was launched in 1996 to address air-pollution problems in Jakarta. It is part of a larger municipal environmental programme, but is in many ways separate from municipal transportation management. The programme includes free testing of vehicle exhaust at a number of locations, the introduction of unleaded gasoline and an effort to increase urban greenery. It also promotes shifting fuel from gasoline to natural gas. Achievements for which the programme takes at least partial credit include an increase in the percentage of vehicles meeting pollution standards, and an increase in the number of natural gas vehicles to 3000 taxis, 500 passenger cars, and 50 public buses by 1997, although the shift began well before 1996.

Leaded gasoline phase-out. In July 2001, the Indonesian oil and gas company Pertamina and the Indonesian government introduced unleaded gasoline sales in greater Jakarta. Indonesia is scheduled to complete its lead phase-out programme by 2003, but this is dependent on completion of various refinery projects. A recent projection is that 80% of the country will be supplied with unleaded gasoline by 2005 (American Embassy, 2001).

Cutting the fuel subsidy. As an oil producing country, Indonesia has traditionally kept the price of oil products in domestic markets below world prices. While no doubt boosting the economy, this policy has probably contributed to the sprawl and car-orientation of Jakarta and other Indonesian cities. An effort to cut the fuel subsidy has had some success, but the prices of gasoline and diesel remain low. A schedule of increases in Indonesian fuel prices over the past decade is presented in Table 4.16.

Table 4.16 Gasoline and Diesel Price Changes
(Price per litre)

Effective Date	Premium Gasoline		Diesel Oil	
	Rupiah	$	Rupiah	$
May 24, 1990	450	$0.05	235	$0.03
July 11, 1991	550	$0.06	285	$0.03
January 8, 1993	700	$0.08	360	$0.04
May 5, 1998	1,200	$0.14	500	$0.06
May 16, 1998	1,000	$0.12	500	$0.06
April, 2000	1,150	$0.13	700	$0.08
October, 2000	1,550	$0.18	900	$0.10
February, 2002	2,000	$0.23	1,200	$0.14

Source : Indonesia 2000, Energy outlook & Statistics;
Note: US$ prices based on June 2002 exchange rate of 8,600 Rupiah per dollar.

Congestion pricing. Many of Jakarta's limited-access highways have been tolled since the 1970s. Tolls implemented before 1997 charge an entry fee ranging from $1 to $2. Recently implemented toll roads charge a kilometre-based fee, ranging from $0.05 to $0.10 per kilometre. As of 1997, there were at least 60 operating or planned toll roads throughout Indonesia. High-occupancy vehicle (HOV) restrictions also exist on some highways.

Planned rail lines and highways. Several multi-billion dollar projects have been proposed for building new transport infrastructure in Jakarta. A major priority for recent governments has been the development of a light-rail system, but none has been initiated to date. Among the most ambitious plans is a metro running under the main north-south corridor through the city, for a distance of 14.5 kilometres. The estimated cost is $2 billion. It would carry an estimated 800 thousand passengers per day (300 million per year) by 2005 and 1.2 million per day (430 million per year) by 2015. A "triple-decker" highway along a major artery has also been proposed.

Opportunities for Bus System Improvements

One of the first steps toward improving bus transport in Jakarta is a bus demonstration project. A key feature of the plan is to improve service without increasing fares or increasing operation subsidies. Limited investment will be combined with operational and organisational changes. The following steps for improving service in one bus corridor have been outlined (Saleh and Haworth, 2000):

■ Identify best location and alignment.

■ Develop plans for infrastructure upgrades, including dedicated bus lanes and better bus stops.

■ Plan appropriate headways and specific timetables for adequate service.

■ Determine services to be licensed and possibly tendered to a private operator.

■ Determine the best form of relationship of the driver and crew to the overseeing company.

Other development guidelines have also been suggested:

■ An entire corridor should be included (not just one bus route on a multi-route corridor) in order to co-ordinate traffic and service on the corridor. The corridor should be a main arterial street. Dedicated bus lanes should be used, preferably in the fast central lanes of the street.

■ The route should allow linkage to other rapid-bus corridors or to an eventual rail network.

■ Bus terminals need to be upgraded to ensure they do not hinder the performance of the demonstration route.

■ Probability of success must be high in order to maximise momentum toward long-term changes.

■ It must be successful in convincing authorities and other interested parties that the approach is better than current practice and can eventually be applied to other parts of the bus system.

■ It must be sufficiently "isolated" from the rest of the system that the costs and benefits associated with it can be identified and measured.

The demonstration project has been divided into three phases, focusing on three different segments of the corridor. A detailed timetable for implementation has been developed (Gadjah Mada, 2001). Actions underway during 2002 include:

- Design of a new regulatory framework for buses.

- Establishment of a new independent bus regulatory body for Jakarta, *Dewan Transportasi Kota*. When established, this body will develop an approach for "quality licensing" of buses.

- Efforts to work with stakeholders and gain their support.

- Presentation of project to Jakarta's legislature, that then will vote whether to approve the project. During 2001, a presentation was made by the Department of Traffic to the Governor, who expressed support for the project.

The estimated cost of the demonstration project for the first phase is $5.8 million. This will include 40 new bus stops, 64 buses, 28 pedestrian bridges and other supporting infrastructure such as walkways and signs.

A potential institutional barrier for this project is opposition from the Private Urban Public Transport Association (Organda). They have indicated opposition because of the potential for the project, and route realignment, to negatively affect their business. It will therefore be important for authorities to work with them to address their concerns and help them to benefit from changes in the current system.

How the Demonstration Bus Project Could be Strengthened

The demonstration project could be strengthened in a number of ways:

- Development of a long term, full-scale plan for bus-rapid transit around the city, to ensure that the demonstration project fits into the longer term plan and that expansion occurs beyond the demonstration phase.

- Adoption of principals for licensing, stakeholder interactions, and route development that have been established by the most successful cities to undertake development of BRT.

- Use of advanced bus system technologies, such as traffic signal priority systems for buses and GPS systems to track buses, pay bus operators, and provide real-time information to riders.

- Purchase of new clean-fuel buses, after undertaking an analysis of what types of buses and fuels make the most sense for Jakarta.

External support and technical assistance could help incorporate these aspects into the project.

MEXICO CITY

Besides being the capital of Mexico, the former Centre of the Aztec empire and, to many, the "Paris" of Latin America, Mexico City has the dubious distinction of being one of the world's most polluted cities. Its dispersed development and large and growing vehicle fleet, combined with its high altitude and mountainous surroundings, make the region susceptible to frequent bouts with dangerously polluted air. Pollutant concentration levels routinely exceed health standards in much of the region. Since the late 1980s, managing air quality in the region has been a top priority for local governments and the focus of much international interest and investment. While some improvements have occurred, little reduction in ambient pollutant concentrations has occurred in the dry season (November to April). The mayor, who took office in late 2000, wants to achieve a real breakthrough in air quality. The challenge is to reduce pollution from all sources and, more importantly, to institute a long-range transport programme that restrains or even reduces car use.

The Mexico City Metropolitan Area (MCMA) is one of the largest urban agglomerations in the world. It covers over 1,500 square kilometres and is home to about 18 million people, roughly 18% of the national population. The MCMA comprises the Federal District (DF) and the surrounding State of Mexico (EDM), which have pursued different transport and environmental strategies. Industrial production is heavily concentrated in the region, accounting for more than 30% of national GDP. But the heaviest and most polluting industries have been pushed out of the Federal District into EDM or beyond, driving population outwards. The city has been growing outwards for decades while population in the city centre has declined slightly. Edge development increased ten-fold between 1970 and 1988 (Sheinbaum and Meyers, 1990).

This growth affects policy-making, since many jurisdictions are now involved in planning Mexico City's policies. As of June 2002, the Mayor's party is different from the party governing the surrounding State of Mexico, while President Fox belongs to a third party. This leads to fractures over many transport and environment issues.

Evolution of the Transport System

The development of transport infrastructure in Mexico City has been very uneven. A trolley strike in the 1910s led to establishment of a privately-owned bus system. In 1945 the city took over the trolley lines. The trolleys gradually gave way to buses and, in 1968, the underground metro system opened. In 1981 the bus system management was transferred to the city under the name "Ruta 100". By 1985, 10,000 buses operated in DF, and Mexico City functioned like other large Latin American cities.

Soon, however, growth in automobile traffic and the expansion of the metro put great strain on the bus system. In response to a declining return on investments in the system, the number of buses was reduced. Internal corruption and growing opposition between the ruling party and individuals with key interests in the bus system led to further downsizing. In 1995 Ruta 100 was declared bankrupt. Many key elements of transport and land-use regulation had simply been ignored, accelerating this collapse (Islas, 1994).

Growing on their own and feeding off disgruntled bus patrons, various kinds of minibuses (called *colectivos,* collective taxis) were welcomed by the government as a way to privatise public transport and reduce government expenditures. Roadway capacity expanded greatly in the 1970s. This, along with the abandonment of investment and maintenance of the public transport system led to a drastic rise in personal vehicle, taxi and *colectivo* use during the 1980s.

By this time the regional bus fleet had dwindled from 15,000 to 2,500. Buses in Mexico City today are run by two companies, Red de Transporte de

Pasajeros (RTP) and Servicios de Transportes Eléctricos (STE). STE still operates the few remaining electric trolleys and tramways and a small number of articulated buses, some on special bus lanes.

As the minibus sector grew, so did corruption and political struggles. Ownership of the minibus fleet (about 50,000 units by 1995) was heavily concentrated among 12 individuals, while minibus production interests were strongly linked to several senators in the city government. The power of the minibus grew over time, and enforcing regulations became increasingly difficult. The city outlawed the production and sale of minibuses in 1995, and a law was passed mandating the conversion of the minibus fleet to standard buses by the end of 1997. This conversion is still taking place very slowly, and only recently have financial terms become favourable enough to allow widespread purchasing of standard buses. Busways are seen as a means of integrating the *colectivos* and the newly-expanded standard bus services. Much debate continues over whether the complete abolition of minibuses would be best for Mexico City.

Mode share has changed dramatically over the past twenty years, as the number of small vehicles has increased. *Colectivos*, which were hardly used until the mid-1980s, now account for over half of all trips. Use of the Metro, which once accounted for 25% of all trips, has fallen by half. Figure 4.3 shows this evolution. Preliminary figures for 2000, supplied by SETRAVI (the Federal District transport authority), show that *colectivos* accounted for more than 55% of all trips, while buses and trolleys carried a mere 10%. In almost every other large Latin American city, buses account for about 50% of all trips.

The present transport system in the MCMA is unusual compared to almost any other city in the developing world. Traffic congestion is notoriously bad during the morning and evening rush hours, and during shopping hours on Saturdays and the return of weekenders on Sunday evening. While there may be cities with worse traffic or higher concentrations of pollutants, Mexico City combines the worst of both.

Figure 4.3 Evolution of Modal Shares of Trips in the MCMA

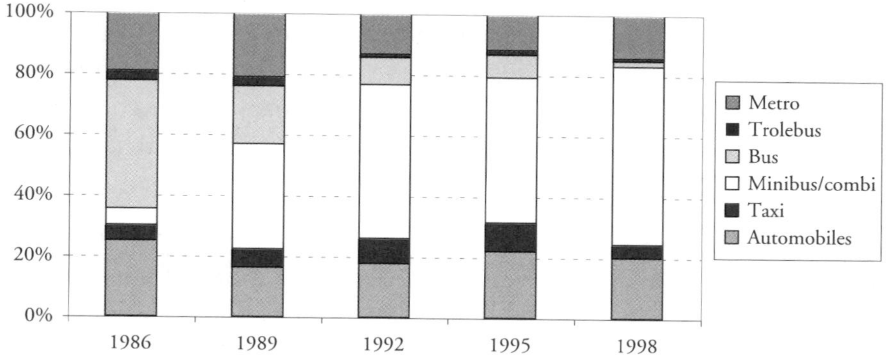

Source: Secretaria de Media Ambiente, based on historical surveys and estimates.

While automobiles or two-wheelers have gained share slowly in virtually every large city in the world, no city shows such a drastic collapse in the share of trips carried by bus and metro as Mexico City.

Travel and Air Pollution Inventory

Concurring estimates of air pollution inventories have been made by various agencies. Most agree reasonably well with each other. The inventory for all sectors in 1998 is shown in Table 4.17.

Table 4.17 Emissions Inventory for the Mexico City Metropolitan Area, 1998
(tonnes per year)

Sector	PM_{10}	SO_2	CO	NO_X	HC
Point sources[a]	3,093	12,442	9,213	26,988	23,980
Area sources[b]	1,678	5,354	25,960	9,866	247,599
Vegetation and ground	7,985	N/A	N/A	3,193	15,669
Mobile sources	7,133	4,670	1,733,663	165,838	187,773
Total	19,889	22,466	1,768,836	205,885	475,021
Mobile source share	35.9%	20.8%	98.0%	80.5%	39.5%

[a] Point sources include large stationary emitters like factories and power plants.

[b] Area sources include small emitters like households and farms.

Source: Government of Mexico City, 2002.

The table shows that transport contributes greatly to local emissions. Mobile sources account for nearly all of the city's CO emissions and about 25% of PM_{10}. NO_x and HCs are important ozone precursors, and most studies conclude that ozone pollution in the region is NO_x-limited, meaning that controls on NO_x would more effectively reduce ozone than controls on VOCs. Transport's high share of NO_x emissions (71%) suggests that reducing this pollutant via transportation measures would be an effective way to reduce ozone formation (Zegras, et al, 2000).

As shown in Table 4.18, each vehicle type makes a different contribution to emissions, depending on its fuel type, efficiency and total kilometres travelled. Colectivos (passenger vans and microbuses) and large buses account for a high percentage of passenger kilometres travelled, but only a modest percentage of transport emissions.

Table 4.18 Transport Mode Shares of Total Emissions, 1998

	PM_{10}	SO_2	CO	NO_X	HC
Private autos	3.5%	8.9%	46.5%	23.0%	17.2%
Taxis	1.0%	2.5%	7.4%	5.4%	3.2%
Combis (passenger vans)	0.1%	0.1%	1.1%	0.5%	0.4%
Colectivos (microbuses)	0.3%	0.7%	12.3%	4.6%	4.2%
Pick-up trucks	0.9%	2.3%	14.4%	9.2%	5.2%
Gasoline trucks	0.4%	1.1%	12.3%	7.4%	3.9%
Diesel vehicles < 3 tonnes	0.7%	0.1%	0.0%	0.1%	0.0%
Tractor trailers (diesel)	10.0%	1.6%	0.9%	11.0%	1.6%
Large buses (diesel)	5.9%	1.0%	0.5%	5.7%	0.8%
Diesel vehicles > 3 tonnes	12.9%	2.1%	1.2%	13.4%	1.9%
LPG freight vehicles/vans	0.1%	0.1%	0.0%	0.2%	0.1%
Motorcycles	0.1%	0.3%	1.3%	0.1%	1.0%
Total transport %	35.9%	20.8%	98.0%	80.6%	39.5%

Source: Government of Mexico City, 2002.

Data taken from the 1996 emissions inventory were used to construct Table 4.19. There is a large difference in the magnitude of travel and emissions between automobiles and *combis* (vans). About 17% of all trips are made by auto and over 50% by *combi*. The automobile pollutes much more than it contributes to the capacity of the system.

[handwritten margin notes: "compare this number for pollution and how much it contributes"]

Table 4.19 Mexico City Transport and Emissions Data, 1998

	Total emissions					Vehicles and travel			Fuel use, gasoline or diesel (million litres)
	SO$_2$ (ktons)	CO (ktons)	NO$_x$ (ktons)	HC (ktons)	PM (ktons)	Fleet size	Average travel per vehicle (km/year)	Total distance (million vehicle-km)	
Private autos	2,000	822,477	47,380	81,705	701	2,341,731	10,329	24,188	3,023
Taxis	567	131,453	11,093	15,310	199	109,407	62,600	6,849	856
Combis (passenger vans)	28	20,448	930	1,945	10	5,499	62,600	344	43
Colectivos (microbuses)	166	216,740	9,524	19,761	59	32,029	62,600	2,005	501
Pick-up trucks	522	255,503	18,961	24,599	183	336,080	18,780	6,312	789
Gasoline trucks	240	216,865	15,297	18,683	84	154,513	18,780	2,902	867
Diesel vehicles < 3 tonnes	24	249	150	168	133	4,733	18,780	89	34
Tractor trailers (diesel)	363	16,675	22,678	7,587	1,990	70,676	18,780	1,327	511
Large buses (diesel)	214	9,270	11,640	3,853	1,174	12,505	62,600	783	301
Diesel vehicles > 3 tonnes	468	20,956	27,662	9,205	2,562	90,940	18,780	1,708	657
LPG freight vehicles/vans	15	298	308	215	16	30,102	18,780	565	N/A
Motorcycles	63	22,729	215	4,742	22	72,704	10,329	751	83

Source: Government of Mexico City, 2002.

Private automobiles are a principal cause of traffic and emissions in the MCMA. The next most important source of overall emissions is trucks, followed by the more than 30,000 *colectivos* (minibuses). There are also roughly 110,000 licensed taxis of varying safety and quality. In contrast, the city has only several thousand public buses.

These figures on mobility, modal split and emissions must be viewed with caution. Although the survey carried out for COMETRAVI by the national Geographic Institute INIGE, is sound, it is difficult to know the real number of trips and length of trip for both vehicles and persons, hence hard to get the baseline of activity level. Fuel use per km is not well known for any fuel-using mode, nor is load factor. These kinds of uncertainties are not trivial, since their resolution is necessary in order for authorities to decide which modes or fuels should be controlled more, and which modes should be encouraged or discouraged.

Various projections show growth in vehicle use evolving relatively slowly over the next 20 years. The Secretary of Transport and Roads (SETRAVI 2002) registered 20.6 million trips in 1994, but foresees only 28.3 million trips in 2020, a decline in per capita terms. While such forecasts are uncertain, any increase in the number of trips means more congestion and pollution unless there is a radical shift away from automobiles and smaller *colectivos,* toward larger capacity vehicles.

Whatever the potential uncertainties in either the emissions factors, or the kilometres, or growth, it is clear that changes in transportation per se will not contribute to reduced air pollution or traffic problems.

Stakeholders in Local Transport Planning and Development

Given the domination of private cars, taxis and *colectivos* on Mexico City's streets, the key actors, representing more than 90% of vehicles, are private individuals, taxi and *colectivo* drivers, and truckers.

The three key public entities are the two bus companies, RTP and STE, and the Metro. STE also operates trams and trolleys. The finances of these organisations are questionable, partly because of stagnant or falling ridership, and their operations are heavily subsidised. However, if fares were raised to better cover costs, more riders might switch to other modes. The efficiency and management of these services has also been criticised, but STE was recently designated as the main operator of proposed tests of advanced buses (discussed below), so it must be included in related policy discussions.

The various regulators and other authorities in the region are also important. The MIT study (Zegras *et al,* 2000) includes an overview of the regional agencies dealing with transportation, land use and air quality. As shown in Table 4.20, there are four levels of government and three main areas of intervention within each.

Table 4.20 Mexican Government Entities Involved in Transportation, Land Use and Environment

	Government entity			
Area	Federal	Federal District	State of Mexico	Mexico City
Transportation	SCT Banobras	SETRAVI	SCT	COMETRAVI
Land use	SEDESOL Banobras	SEDUVI	SEDUOP	COMETAH
Environment	SEMARNAP (INE, Profepa)	SMA	SE	CAM

Source: MIT report (Zegras et al, 2000).

Since the transportation and air quality problems in the MCMA are inherently regional, it is unfortunate – though not unusual for large cities – that attempts to "regionalise" institutional structures in these sectors has been slow. In the 1980s, two regional bodies were formed, one dealing specifically with metro area air quality (The Metropolitan Environmental Commission or CAM) and the other with transportation (The Metropolitan Commission for Transport and Roadways or COMETRAVI). Despite similar mandates for handling their respective sectors, CAM has access to independent financial resources (the Fideicomiso Ambiental, an environmental trust fund), while COMETRAVI does not. Further, CAM has executive and regulatory powers, while COMETRAVI's powers are essentially of a consultative and proposal-making nature.

Vehicle manufacturers are an important force in the region. The major vehicle manufacturers in Mexico City include Ford, GM, Nissan and Renault, each making light-duty vehicles; and Mercedes/Freightliner, International, Volvo, and Scania making buses and/or heavy vehicles. They have been active in the past in discussions about pollution and vehicle emissions, but they do not appear to have played a strong role in policy-making. However, in part because of the North American Free Trade

Agreement zone, more than half of Mexican motor vehicle production is now exported. The manufacturers have a strong incentive to push to improve environmental standards in Mexico so the same vehicles made for the Mexican market can be sold in Canada and the US as well.

Pemex, the national oil company, has a virtual monopoly on the sale of all oil products. They have shown interest in participating in experiments with alternative fuels and low-sulphur diesel fuel (their present fuel is relatively clean by international standards, 350 ppm sulphur). Pemex could play a pivotal role in testing and implementing clean fuels. It is controlled by the National Government's Ministry of Finance, and relations with the region at the working level appear good.

Recent Initiatives

During the past decade air quality management programmes have focussed on cleaning up vehicles at the tailpipe and cleaning up fuels. Unfortunately, as in Los Angeles, where much cleaner vehicles now drive much, much more, results have been less than impressive. Vehicle fuel intensity and extent of vehicle use must also be addressed in order to make significant progress. This includes increasing average vehicle occupancy by moving ridership out of *colectivos* and into full-size buses. About 40% of vehicles are more than 10 years old and have no emission controls. Operation of these older vehicles is restricted under the *Hoy no Circúla* policy (see below). No other strict traffic policy is being considered, judging from SETRAVI's draft 2002 plan covering the period 2002-2006.

The 2002 plan contains many familiar elements, but some new ones as well. SETRAVI acknowledges that the transport sector needs profound institutional reform. It de-emphasises *colectivos*, and targets more travel in larger vehicles, although it identifies a continued role for *colectivos*, as feeders from dispersed areas (or areas without wide streets) towards the main bus and metro lines. It also recognises that the *colectivos* speed and convenience is a factor in winning them high market share from the metro and bus lines. Clearly the service from large buses must improve in order to win ridership back.

SETRAVI's 2002-2006 programme includes the following elements:

- Improving the transport regulations in the Federal District.

- Developing public transportation corridors, including new busways as well as efforts to substitute large buses for *colectivos* on some existing routes.

- Retrofitting some existing vehicles for alternative fuels.

- Renewal of the ageing taxi fleet.

- Modernisation of the ticketing system for the Metro.

A recent project announced by the World Bank, the World Resources institute and the Shell Foundation, as discussed below, will provide substantial resources to support these efforts.

Buses and Busways

The city is focusing on buses and facilities for buses in its medium range transportation planning. A study of potential approaches was conducted in 1999 by SETRAVI. The study identified 33 corridors adequate travel demand and other characteristics needed for use as busways. The busway project was partly motivated by the plan to restrict the operation of *colectivos* and replace them with small and medium-size buses. Perhaps surprisingly, the *colectivo* organisation sees moving to larger vehicles as a good thing for its operators' futures. Thus there may be good support for changes in this direction. However, care must be taken to avoid simply replacing *colectivos* with slower and less frequent buses. This could backfire, especially by losing ridership among the car-owning *colectivo* users.

The bus company RTP took delivery in 2001 of 250 buses compliant with 1998 US EPA standards. Although not as clean as new buses in OECD countries are in 2002, these buses will pollute significantly less than standard buses in the fleet. Several new bus routes have been designated that integrate with the Metro. RTP currently has 860 operating buses in its fleet, with 665 in service on the street. This fleet carries about 450,000 trips per work day.

Servicio de Transportes Electricos, under its new director Dr. Florencia Serrania, recently began increased bus service on *Eje Central*, a main north-south route from the city's historical centre, using single bus-only lanes in both directions. Bus frequency was increased from every 20 minutes to every 3.5 minutes during peak periods. Ridership increased by 35% on this line in the first two weeks, with no publicity except word of mouth. Currently negotiating with the police for better enforcement of the bus-only lanes, STE believes this low cost experiment could be the beginning of an important renaissance of the region's bus system, using fast buses running in protected corridors.

Fuel Conversion

Fuel improvements were a central part of earlier air quality management measures. The move to unleaded gasoline, the adoption of catalytic converters and the adoption of US Tier I light-duty vehicle emission standards have all contributed to the recent decrease in vehicle emissions. The sulphur content of diesel fuels has also been lowered, reducing sulphur dioxide emissions. Early programmes to convert vehicles to liquid petroleum gas (LPG) were not entirely successful. In 1992, only one percent of the vehicle fleet ran on LPG as the result of roughly 600 conversions at a cost of 60,000 pesos each. More recently, thousands of light freight vehicles and *colectivos* have been converted, spurred in part by low LPG prices. Still, major disincentives for conversion remain in 2002, including lack of filling stations. Stations are located only in a few industrial areas. Rightly or wrongly, individuals and the authorities are concerned about the safety of LPG, which is one reason why pumps are in isolated areas. Vehicle conversions are not always high quality, and LPG in Mexico is of mixed quality, with wide variations in the butane/propane proportions.

The use of compressed natural gas (CNG) for vehicles has been increasing. Spurred by large investments by French and Spanish gas companies, a strategy for constructing CNG stations is developing, although not many are yet in place. A subsidiary of the French company Maxigas, called Ecovehicular, plans substantial fuel infrastructure development and programmes to encourage light and medium vehicles to switch to CNG.

Gasoline quality has not gone unnoticed. The federal Proaire programme, begun in 1996, stipulated the introduction of a premium PEMEX gasoline grade with greater oxygenate content. Methyl tertiary butyl ether (MTBE) has been used in gasoline since 1989. Roughly 85% of all gasoline sold in the MCMA is actually produced in a Shell/Pemex Refinery in Deer Park, Texas, because of its high quality.

Overall local emissions per kilometre by vehicle type are lower in 2002 than in 1992, the year when tough tailpipe standards were introduced. Whether the air in 2002 is significantly cleaner than in 1992 is unclear, although there are fewer days when the norms for CO, NO_x and ozone are exceeded.

Traffic-related Initiatives

The following are among the major traffic-related initiatives in recent years.

Hoy no Circúla. A major policy affecting automobiles is Hoy No Circúla (HNC), involving day-of-week vehicle driving restrictions. It was imposed in 1989 as a part of the short-term emergency programme for the winter months in Mexico City. Based on the last digit of the license plate, 20% of all private vehicles were banned on each weekday. The aim of the programme is to reduce congestion, pollution and fuel consumption by reducing total vehicle travel. Studies from that first winter indicated that fuel consumption did decrease while metro ridership and average vehicle speeds increased (Onursal & Gautam, 1997). When the first major air-pollution control plan (PICCA) was deployed in 1990 with a five-year time horizon, *Hoy No Circúla* was a major component. Later analyses, however, indicated that the long-term impacts of the programme are debatable (Eskeland & Feyzioglu, 1997). A large number of used vehicles have been imported into the Mexico City area in recent years, suggesting that many families have added a car to their household in order to circumvent the rule. Whether it has any appreciable impact any more is unclear. In any case new vehicles are now exempt so this policy appears likely to fade away over time.

Segundo Piso. In December 2001 the Mayor announced a new plan that aims to double the capacity of the main ring road around the city[18], by adding a second deck. While the plan has come under attack from many groups, it offers the mayor a chance to consolidate many other elements of environment and transport policy into one package. As of June 2002 the plan was on hold, with the first round of contractor bids rejected as too expensive, and continued strong opposition.

---

18 Known as *El Periferico*; see http://www.segundonivel.df.gob.mx/

International Agency-led Initiatives

Two important initiatives are underway led by international agencies. The United Nations Development Program and the Global Environmental Facility have approved a project to put up to eight fuel-cell buses in Mexico city (with similar projects in Sao Paulo and four other cities around the developing world). This project will also fund development of hydrogen refuelling infrastructure, using natural gas line as the fuel supply. The local agent will be the bus company STE, with the National Autonomous University of Mexico acting as the technical advisor. The project will run the test buses in bus corridors (being planned) to ensure that the world's most valuable vehicles are not stuck in traffic most of the time.

A complementary initiative led by the World Bank and EMBARQ (operated by the World Resources Institute and funded by the Shell Foundation) will put a number of different clean-fuel buses into operation in Mexico City. These will include low-sulphur diesel, diesel hybrid, LPG and compressed natural gas. This project will include emissions testing and comparisons of bus performance, costs, and passenger reactions[19].

Both projects include development of rapid bus corridors or busways. A related busway project being considered by SETRAVI would prioritise the use of newer buses on the busway and attempt to arrange careful testing of these buses. Efforts will also be made to encourage *colectivo* drivers to provide feeder service to these corridors. Other stakeholders such as merchants along the routes will be involved. Overall, the project will test the ability of all involved partners to build these two projects into a wider strategy of sustainable transport and environmental policy. As a key step in the process, a large engineering study is being undertaken during 2002 to develop a more detailed design and implementation plan for the busways (Urbanismo y Sistemas de Transporte, SA de CV, 2001).

Assessment and Potential Near-term Strategy

If long-term air quality, energy use, and CO_2 emissions goals are to be met, the focus on making vehicles cleaner must shift to making the system itself cleaner, and this is beginning to occur. In fact vehicles and fuels have been cleaned up from earlier levels, although there are still gains to be made in

---

19 For more information about EMBARQ, see http://www.embarq.org/

this area. New vehicles, especially large vehicles and buses, are beginning to meet the latest European and US emissions standards. Official recognition of the role of *colectivos* would permit authorities to move them more rapidly to cleaner fuels. Only by offering car users a decent alternative can travel policies that restrict car use (like *Hoy no Circúla*) really be effective and fair.

Doing this will be difficult. Mexico City must develop and carry out an overall transport plan, not just an emissions reduction plan. A key aspect will be re-invigorating public transit systems, especially buses, so that they provide much better service than they do currently. But other steps must be take as well. Issues of land use and the endless sprawl of the metro area must be addressed, and policies that discourage car use (such as stricter parking laws) may be needed. The private sector should be involved in discussions at all stages, and public support for what amounts to an alternative transport and land-use paradigm must be generated, if Mexico City is to make significant progress.

Many positive changes are beginning to take place in Mexico City. The new local government appears ready to implement strong measures for both transportation and emissions reductions. The transportation department, SETRAVI, is actively developing plans for busways, and international support is being provided to test a variety of bus technologies on the new routes. The local government seems open to reconsidering the role of the *colectivos* in the overall transport system, while acknowledging that they provide a useful service. Pemex and the vehicle manufacturers appear ready to move to cleaner fuels and technologies, although more testing and development work still must be carried out.

Developing pilot projects will be helpful in the effort to push forward along the path of the city's long-range transport strategy. The World Bank/GEF/Shell Foundation project proposed a number of strategies with the pilot bus corridor project lying at the centre. In order to ensure that this first corridor lays a strong foundation for future expansion of rapid, clean transit services, it should include:

- Dedicated bus corridors, with strong physical separation from other traffic lanes.

- Modern bus stops, bus ticketing, and advanced rider information systems – especially pre-board ticketing and multi-door buses to ensure rapid boarding and alighting.

- Integrated ticketing that allows free transfers across transit companies and modes (bus, tram and Metro) and, if possible, including *colectivos* in this system.

- Differentiated services such as express services, or premium services at higher fares.

- Testing of advanced technology buses (e.g. hybrids, as well as the fuel-cell buses that will be provided by the UNDP programme), low floor or articulated buses, and alternative fuels and low-sulphur diesel.

- Formal co-ordination with *colectivo* operators to create new feeder services to the bus stations, with opportunities for integrating fares between the modes.

- Develop a new regime for bus licensing, regulation and compensation on this corridor – emulating the "quality licensing" programmes of cities like Bogota.

- Strengthening methods of enforcement and evaluation.

- Building a strong network of pedestrian and cycle access to busway and metro stations.

- Renovating areas around busway stations to create vibrant, pedestrian-oriented neighbourhoods, as has been achieved in cities like Bogota and Quito.

- Land-use reform to encourage higher densities around busway stations.

BIBLIOGRAPHY

American Embassy, 2001, "The Petroleum Report: Indonesia 2001", Jakarta.

APTA, 1999. *Transit Vehicle Data Book*, American Public Transit Association.

ARCO, 2001, "EC Diesel program summary", http://ecdiesel.com/programdata.html.

Barnes, Allyson, *et al*, 2000, "Evaluation of Water-blend Fuels in a City Bus and an Assessment of Performance with Emission Control Devices", Society of Automotive Engineers paper SAE 2000-01-1915.

BP Amoco, 2001, Corporate Information, http://www.dmeforpower.net/brief-India.pdf.

Bogota Project, 2000, http://ecoplan.org/votebogota2000/vb2_index.htm.

Bose, Ranjan, and Daniel Sperling, 2001, "Transportation in Developing Countries: Greenhouse Gas Scenarios for Delhi, India", published by Pew Centre on Global Climate Change, Arlington VA.

Canada, 2001, "Dimethyl Ether Fuel System Studies", Transport Canada (in cooperation with Natural Resources Canada), http://www.tc.gc.ca/tdc/projects/road/e/9361.htm2000.

CARB, 2000, "CARB Fuels Report, Diesel Risk Reduction Plan", Appendix IV, October 2000, California Air Resource Board, http://www.arb.ca.gov/diesel/documents/rrpapp4.PDF.

Cervero, Robert, 1998, *The Transit Metropolis: A Global Inquiry*, Island Press, Washington DC.

CFCP (California Fuel Cell Partnership), 2001, "Bringing Fuel Cells To Market, Scenarios and Challenges with Fuel Alternatives".

COMETRAVI, 1999. Volumes 1-8 of *Estudio Integral de Transporte y Calidad del Aire en la Zona Metropolitana del Valle de México*.

Contrans/CIRT, 1999, *Bangalore MetroBus Feasibility Study*, for Bangalore Metropolitan Transport Corp. (BMTC) and Swedish International Development Cooperation Agency (SIDA).

Curitiba, 2001, Information from city website, http://www.curitiba.pr.gov.br/pmc/ingles/Solucoes/Transporte/index.html.

DeCicco, John, 2001, "Technology Status and Commercialisation Prospects of Fuel Cells for Highway Vehicles", American Council for an Energy Efficient Economy.

Detroit Diesel, 2000, "Detroit Diesel unveils year 2000 Series 50 bus and coach engine", http://www.detroitdiesel.com/public/corp/031700bus.asp.

DITS, 1994, *Greater Dhaka Metropolitan Area Integrated Transport Study, Final Report*, Planning Commission and Department of Economic and Social Development, Government of Bangladesh and United Nations Development Program.

Dieselnet, 2000, http://www.dieselnet.com/news/0007hk.html.

Dorsch *et al*, 1998, "Surabaya Integrated Transport Network Project, Report B3: Traffic Demand Management".

ECMT, 2001, "Vehicle Emission Reductions", European Conference of Ministers of Transport, OECD/ECMT, Paris.

ENGVA, 2001, *Statistics 2001*, European Natural Gas Vehicle Association.

Eskeland & Feyzioglu, 1997, "Rationing Can Backfire: The 'Day without a Car' in Mexico City", *The World Bank Economic Review*, Vol. 11, No. 3.

EU, 2000, "Sagittaire Hybrid Vehicle Demonstration Project", European Commission, http://europa.eu.int/comm/energy_transport/en/prog_cut_en.html.

FTA (Federal Transit Administration), 2002, "BRT Reference Guide: Land Use Policy", Federal Transit Administration, US DOT, http://www.fta.dot.gov/brt/guide/landuse.html.

FTA, 2002b, "Bus Rapid Transit Demonstration Projects", Federal Transit Administration, US DOT, http://www.fta.dot.gov/brt/projects/index.html.

FTA, 2001, Federal Transit Administration, "Issues in Bus Transit", http://www.fta.dot.gov/brt/issues/pt1.html (through pt5.html).

FTA, 2000, "Hybrid-Electric Transit Buses: Status, Issues, and Benefits", Transit Co-operative Research Program, TCRP Report 59.

GAO, 2001, "Mass Transit: Bus Rapid Transit Shows Progress", US General Accounting Office, Washington DC.

Gadjah Mada, 2001, "Academic Manuscript for Operate Urban Public Transport Centre", Transportation Studies, Gadjah Mada University, Indonesia.

Georgetown, 2000, *Advanced Vehicle Development Program*, Georgetown University, Washington DC.

GM (General Motors), 2000, GM Press Release, August 10.

Gopalan, Murali, 1999, "BP-Amoco mulls tie-up with IOC, Gail for mega fuel-supply project," *Financial Express*, November 1.

Gordon, P. *et al*, 1999, "Improving Transportation in the San Fernando Valley", Reason Public Policy Institute, RPPI Policy Study 249.

Government of Mexico City, 2002, "Emissions Inventory", Secretaria de Media Ambiente.

Halcrow Fox, 2000, "World Bank Urban Transport Strategy Review – Mass Rapid Transit in Developing Countries", Final Report, Department for International Development, World Bank.

Hansen, J.B. and Mikkelsen, S.E., 2001, "DME as a Transportation Fuel", Reported by Haldor Topsøe A/S for The Danish Road Safety and Transport Agency and the Danish Environmental Protection Agency, Lyngby, July.

Henscher, David A, 1999, "A Bus-Based Transitway or Light Rail? Continuing the Saga on Choice v. Blind Commitment", *Road and Transport Research*, Vol 8:3, September 1999.

Holmén, Britt, Alberto Ayala, Norman Kado and Robert Okamoto, 2001, "ARB's Study of Emissions from 'Late-model' Diesel and CNG Heavy-duty Transit Buses", presented at the Fifth International ETH Conference on Nanoparticle Measurements, August 6-8, Zürich.

Hong Kong, 1999, Policy Address, Government of Hong Kong, http://www.info.gov.hk/pa99/english/part5-1.htm.

Hong Kong, 2000, Description of air quality improvement program, Government of Hong Kong, http://www.info.gov.hk/hk2000/eng/16/c16-03_content.htm.

Hosier, Richard, 2000, "Commercialisation of Fuel Cell Buses: Potential Roles for the Global Environment Facility (GEF)", UNDP, April.

IEA, 2000, *World Energy Outlook 2000*, International Energy Agency, Paris.

IEA/AFIS, 1999, *Automotive Fuels for the Future*, International Energy Agency, Paris.

INFORM, 2000, *Bus Futures: New Technologies for Cleaner Cities*, INFORM, Inc.

ITDP, 2001, "Cuenca Gets On The Bus" *Sustainable Transport*, number 12, Fall 2001, Institute for Transportation and Development Policy,

Johnson Matthey, 2000, Corporate information - Catalytic Systems Division, http://www.jmcsd.com/html/arco.html.

Johnson Matthey, 2001, Information on CRT system, http://www.jmcsd.com/crt912.pdf.

Jupiter, 2000, Jupiter-2 Project Description (Joint Urban Project in Transport Energy Reduction, European Commission), Energy Directorate, http://www.jupiter-2.net/ihome.htm.

Kenworthy, Jeffrey R., and Felix B. Laube, 1999, "Patterns of automobile dependence in cities: an international overview of key physical and economic dimensions with some implications for urban policy", *Transportation Research Part A*, v33, pp691-723.

LACMTA, 1999, "Fuel Strategies for Future Bus Procurements, Final Report", Los Angeles County Metro Transportation Authority, August.

LA, 2001, "Los Angeles Transit Priority System Evaluation Report", City of Los Angeles Department of Transportation.

Lanni et al., 2001, "Results of NYCT Diesel Bus Emissions Tests", Society of Automotive Engineers, SAE Paper #2001-01-05110.

Levelton, 1999, "Alternative and Future Fuels and Energy Sources for Road Vehicles", Report for Transportation Issue Table, National Climate Change Process, prepared by Levelton Engineering Ltd, Richmond B.C., http://www.tc.gc.ca/envaffairs/subgroups1/vehicle_technology/study1/final_report/part1-4/final_report.htm.

Lloyd, Alan C. and Thomas A. Cackette, 2001, "Diesel Engines: Environmental Impact and Control", Journal of Air and Waste Management, Volume 51, June 2001.

Los Alamos National Laboratory, 1999, *Fuel Cells: Green Power*, Shimshon Gottesfeld.

Lubrizol, 2001, Corporate press release, February 1, and other corporate materials, http://www.lubrizol.com/news/2001/0202-carb.htm.

Lubrizol, 2002, Fuel quality "Ready Reference", http://www.lubrizol.com/ReadyReference/GasolineDieselFuels/lzgasspecs.htm.

MATES (*Multiple Air Toxics Exposure Study II*), 1999, South Coast Air Quality Management District, Diamond Bar, CA, http://www.aqmd.gov/news1/MATES_II_results.htm.

Meakin, Richard, 2000, "Pilot Corridor Bus Improvements Project: Legal, Policy, and Institutional Aspects", Sustainable Urban Transport Project, Surabaya.

MECA, 2001, "Emission Control Retrofit of Existing Diesel Engines", in *Clean Air Facts*, Manufacturers of Emission Controls Association.

MECA, 2000, "Catalyst-Based Diesel Particulate Filters and NO_x Adsorbers: A Summary of the Technologies and the Effects of Fuel Sulphur", Manufacturers of Emission Controls Association.

MECA, 2000b, "Emission Control Retrofit of Diesel-Fuelled Vehicles," March 2000.

MECA, 1999, "Demonstration of Advanced Emission Control Technologies Enabling Diesel-powered Heavy-duty Engines to Achieve Low Emission Levels".

Meirelles, Alexandre, 2000, "A Review of Bus Priority Systems in Brazil: from Bus Lanes to Busway Transit", Smart Urban Transport Conference, 17-20 October 2000, Brisbane Australia.

NAVC, 2000, "Hybrid-Electric Drive Heavy-duty Vehicle Testing Project, Final Emissions Report", Northeast Advanced Vehicle Consortium, Boston, February 15.

NAVC, Advanced Vehicle Consortium, 2000b, "Future Wheels: Interviews with 44 Global Experts On the Future of Fuel Cells for Transportation And Fuel Cell Infrastructure", prepared by M.J. Bradley and Associates.

NAVC, 1999, "Comparison of Emissions Performance for Alternative Fuelled (CNG) and Conventional Fuelled Heavy-Duty Transit Buses", Northeast Alternative Vehicle Consortium, June.

Neilson, Gordon, 2000, "Improving Public Transport in Surabaya Through a Demonstration Route", GTZ, Sustainable Urban Transport Project, http://www.sutp.org/docs.

NYCTRC (NY City Transit Riders Council), 2000, "Analysis of Alternative Fuel Technologies for New York City Transit Buses", February.

NYCT (NY City Transit, Dept. of Buses), 2000, "NYCT Operating Experience with Hybrid Transit Buses", Presentation at SAE International Truck and Bus Meeting, Portland, OR, Dec 4-6 2000. Slides provided by Dana Lowell, NYCT.

NYS-DEC et al, 2001, "Emissions Results from Clean Diesel Demonstration Program with CRT™ Particulate Filter at New York City Transit", presentation, New York State DEC MTA, NYCT, Johnson Matthey, Equilon, Corning, Environment Canada, and RAD Energy, available from Dana Lowell, NYCT.

Onursal, B. & S. Gautum, 1997, "Vehicular Air Pollution: Experiences from Seven Latin American Urban Centres", World Bank Technical Paper No. 373, Washington, DC.

Penn State, 2001, Penn State Institute News, August 27.

Penalosa, Enrique (former mayor of Bogota), 2002, "Appropriate Transport for the Third World City", in Urban Transport for Growing Cities, ed. G. Tiwari, Macmillan India Ltd.

Rabinowitch, J. and J. Leitman, 1993, "Environmental Innovation and Management in Curitiba, Brazil". Washington DC, UNCP/UNCHS World Bank Urban Management Programme, Working Paper #1.

RATP, 2001, "Bilan des Experimentations Bus Ecologiques", Document de Synthese, RATP, Paris.

Rebelo, Jorge M. and Pedro P. Benvenuto, 1995, "Concessions of Busways to the Private Sector: the Sao Paulo Experience", World Bank.

Reddy, Dr C P and Prasad, Dr C M V Prasad, 2000, "Wear Characteristics of a Four-stroke Diesel Engine Through Endurance Tests with Diesel and Water-diesel Emulsions", MC0907 Mechanical Journal, September.

Ristola, Tomi, 2000, "Overview of Current Implementations of Passenger Information Technology", Infopolis-2 Project, University of Limerick, Ireland.

Saleh, Ir. Hasan Basri, and Dr. Sion Haworth, 2000, "Transport Demand Management and Bus Reform in Jakarta", Presented at the International Conference on Sustainable Transport & Clean Air, Jakarta, 29-31 May.

Sari, Agus, and Bambang Susantono, 1999, "The Blue Sikes Initiatives: Voluntary Actions to Reduce Urban and Global Air Pollution in Jakarta", Pelangi Indonesia, Jakarta.

Schipper, Lee, Celine Marie-Lilliu and Roger Gorham, 2000, "Flexing the Link Between Transport and Greenhouse Gas Emissions: A Path for the World Bank", World Bank publications, Washington DC.

Schodel, H., 1999, "Thirty Five years of Experience with LPG Buses", Vienna Transport Association, Vienna, presented at European Bus and Clean Fuel Summit, London, September 1999.

SETRAVI, 1999, *Study for Bus-Colectivo Substitution Program and 33 Bus Corridors.*

Sheinbaum, C. and Meyers, S., 1995. "Transportation in Mexico City". *Energy for Sustainable Development,* Volume 2, No. 3.

STM, 2000, *PITU 2020,* Sao Paulo State Secretary for Metropolitan Transports, http://www.stm.sp.gov.br/ingesp/english.html.

Sunline Transit Agency, 2001, "Today's Model for Tomorrow's World", Coachella Valley, CA.

SUTP, 2002, *Sustainable Urban Transport Project,* GTZ, Surabaya http://www.sutp.org/.

TERI, 2001, "Delhi's Transport and the Environment: Shaken but not Stirred", Tata Energy Research Institute, Delhi, http://www.teriin.org/energy/delhi.htm#tab3.

UK, 2000, "Report of the Alternative Fuels Group of the Cleaner Vehicles Task Force" (government/industry combined authorship).

US DOE (Department of Energy), 2000, Office of Transportation Technologies, "Impact of Diesel Fuel Sulphur on CIDI Emission Control Technology", August.

US DOE (Department of Energy), 2000b, Office of Transportation Technologies, "Diesel Emission Control: Sulphur Effects (DECSE) Program Phase II Summary Report: NO_x Adsorber Catalysts" (October).

US DOE (Department of Energy), 2001, "Dimethyl Ether Use in a 4-Cylinder Diesel Engine", *Advanced Automotive Technologies Report.*

US EIA (Energy Information Administration), 2001, "The Transition to Ultra-Low-Sulphur Diesel Fuel: Effects on Prices and Supply".

US EPA, 2000b, Regulatory Impact Analysis, Heavy Duty Engine and Vehicle Standards and Highway Diesel Fuel Sulphur Control Requirements, Environmental Protection Agency, December, EPA 420-R-00-026, http://www.epa.gov/otaq/diesel.htm.

US EPA, 2000, *Technical Support Document for the Heavy-Duty Engine and Vehicle Standards and Highway Diesel Fuel Sulphur Control Requirements: Air Quality Modelling Analyses,* EPA 420-R-00-028, December.

UNDP (United Nations Development Program), 2001, Press Release, "Global fuel cell bus project offers relief for sprawling mega cities", http://www.undp.org/dpa/pressrelease/releases/2001/october/1oct01.html.

UCS (Union of Concerned Scientists), 2000, "Cleaner Transit: New Buses", http://www.ucsusa.org/vehicles/cleantransit.html.

URBAIR, 1997, "Urban Air Quality Management Strategy in Asia: Jakarta Report", Jitendra Shah, Tanvi Nagpal, and Carter J. Brandon, editors, World Bank Technical Paper No. 379, Washington DC.

Urbanismo y Sistemas de Transporte, SA de CV, 2001, *Proposta Preliminar: Deseño Functional y Projecto del Corridor Eje Central.*

Ventura County, 2001, "Ventura County Fare Integration: A Case Study", ITS Cooperative Deployment Network, US FTA/FHWA, http://www.nawgits.com/fhwa/.

Volvo *et al,* 2002, "Final Draft: The Bio-DME Project, Phase 1", Report to Swedish National Energy Administration (STEM).

Volvo, 1998, "Alternative Fuels: A compilation of facts and the view that Volvo Truck Corporation takes on some types of fuel", Volvo Truck Corp., Sweden.

WBCSD, 2001, *Mobility 2001*, World Business Council for Sustainable Development, Sustainable Mobility Working Group, prepared by MIT and Charles River Associates.

Wirth, C., 1997. "Transportation Policy in Mexico City", *Urban Affairs Review,* Vol 33, no 2.

World Bank, 2001, *Cities on the Move: A World Bank Urban Transport Strategy Review,* consultation draft, available at http://wbln0018.worldbank.org/transport/utsr.nsf.

World Bank, 1996, *Sustainable Transport: Priorities for Policy Reform,* Washington, DC.

Wright, Lloyd, 2002, "Latin American Busways: Moving People Rather than Cars", in *Urban Transport for Growing Cities*, ed. G. Tiwari, Macmillan India Ltd.

WLPGA, 2001, World LP Gas Association, *Statistics 2001.*

Xcellsis, Ballard Power Systems, *et al,* 2001, "Cleaning Up: Zero Emission Buses in Real World Use", A Report on the Xcellsis/Ballard Phase 3 Fuel Cell Bus Program.

Xie, Jiang, Jitendra Shah and Carter Brandon, 1998, "Fighting Urban Transport Air Pollution for Local and Global Good: The Case of Two-stroke Engine Three Wheelers in Delhi", World Bank.

Xie, J., C. Brandon, and J. Shah, 1998b, "Fighting Urban Transport Air Pollution for Local and Global Good: The Case of Two Stroke Engine Three Wheelers in Dhaka", The World Bank.

Zegras, C. *et al.,* 2000. "Metropolitan Mexico City Mobility & Air Quality", White Paper for the MIT Integrated Program on Urban, Regional and Global Air Pollution.

ORDER FORM

IEA BOOKS

Fax: +33 (0)1 40 57 65 59
E-mail: books@iea.org
www.iea.org/books

INTERNATIONAL ENERGY AGENCY

9, rue de la Fédération
F-75739 Paris Cedex 15

I would like to order the following publications

PUBLICATIONS	ISBN	QTY	PRICE		TOTAL
☐ Bus Systems for the Future - Achieving Sustainable Transport Worldwide	92-64-19806-7		US$100	€110	
☐ World Energy Outlook - 2001 Insights	92-64-19658-7		US$150	€165	
☐ World Energy Outlook - 2002	92-64-19835-0		US$150	€165	
☐ Coal in the Energy Supply of India	92-64-19799-0		US$80	€88	
☐ Saving Oil and Reducing CO_2 Emissions in Transport - Options & Strategies	92-64-19519-X		US$125	€137	
☐ The Road from Kyoto - Current Co_2 & Transport Policies in the IEA	92-64-18561-5		US$75	€82	
☐ Energy Technology and Climate Change - A Call to Action	92-64-18563-1		US$75	€82	
☐ Toward a Sustainable Energy Future	92-64-18688-3		US$50	€55	
			TOTAL		

DELIVERY DETAILS

Name   Organisation

Address

Country   Postcode

Telephone   E-mail

PAYMENT DETAILS

☐ I enclose a cheque payable to IEA Publications for the sum of $ _____ or € _____

☐ Please debit my credit card (tick choice).   ☐ Mastercard   ☐ VISA   ☐ American Express

Card no: ⌞_____⌟

Expiry date: ⌞_____⌟   Signature:

OECD PARIS CENTRE
Tel: (+33-01) 45 24 81 67
Fax: (+33-01) 49 10 42 76
E-mail: distribution@oecd.org

OECD BONN CENTRE
Tel: (+49-228) 959 12 15
Fax: (+49-228) 959 12 18
E-mail: bonn.contact@oecd.org

OECD MEXICO CENTRE
Tel: (+52-5) 280 12 09
Fax: (+52-5) 280 04 80
E-mail: mexico.contact@oecd.org

You can also send your order to your nearest OECD sales point or through the OECD online services:
www.oecd.org/bookshop

OECD TOKYO CENTRE
Tel: (+81-3) 3586 2016
Fax: (+81-3) 3584 7929
E-mail: center@oecdtokyo.org

OECD WASHINGTON CENTER
Tel: (+1-202) 785-6323
Toll-free number for orders:
(+1-800) 456-6323
Fax: (+1-202) 785-0350
E-mail: washington.contact@oecd.org

IEA PUBLICATIONS, 9, rue de la Fédération, 75739 PARIS CEDEX 15
Pre-press and cover LINÉALE PRODUCTION
Printed in France by SAGIM-CANALE
(61 02 26 1 P1) ISBN 92-64-19806-7 – 2002